A Chip Off the Silicon Block

The Power of Entrepreneurial Thinking

Carol Latham

PAGE PUBLISHING, INC.
Conneaut Lake, PA

First originally published by Page Publishing 2020

ISBN 978-1-64584-837-0 (pbk)
ISBN 978-1-64584-839-4 (hc)
ISBN 978-1-64584-838-7 (digital)

Printed in the United States of America

For my sons, Jim and Craig, who made the ultimate commitment of their budding careers to join my entrepreneurial adventure and contributed selflessly to our success.

C O N T E N T S

The Turn of the Century

Life After Thermagon

A C K N O W L E D G M E N T S

Selling our products is like shooting fish in a barrel.

—Gregory Blair, Thermagon employee

Once convinced that creating a record of my entrepreneurial experience could have value for myself, as well as for others who are searching for their own entrepreneurial adventure, I cleared my desk, sat down, booted up my computer, and began to write. My knowledge of the ins and outs of writing and publishing a book could be compared to what the average person knows about rocket science—very little. Nevertheless, I proceeded to write my story down word by word and paragraph by paragraph.

It was not until several chapters deep that someone suggested I should find an editor to review my document. Lo and behold, an editor emerged from my son's extended family, someone who graciously consented to review my work. It is with much gratitude and thanks that I acknowledge Anne Marie Nicholson for her work in editing this book and giving me the confidence to continue. Also, I want to thank my friend Kathy Roulston who showed unwavering enthusiasm for my work and would sit intently listening as I would read my story aloud as it unfolded. This enthusiasm gave me the courage and strength to continue. Thank you, Kathy!

Not until I finished the last chapter of this book did I realize that I was entering unchartered territory about which I knew very little. I began asking every friend and acquaintance that I encountered if they knew anyone who had knowledge or experience on how to publish my document. And that is how I found Natalie June Reilly, an author and prolific writer, who transformed my document into this book. To her, I will be forever grateful. Thank you, Natalie.

In order to complete the last chapter of this book, which brings my story forward to today, I reached out to the current Laird employees who were part of my team when the company was sold. They graciously consented to a conversation with me to share their work experiences over the past fifteen years that they spent as part of Laird. I am proud of each and every one of them and their contribution to the success of the thermal material business. I extend my thanks to Kevin Bohrer, Karen Bruzda, Brisha Conway, Tuesday Hale, Yuqin Li, Joseph Nicholson, Mistelina Quinones, Luz Rivera, Yolanda Ruiz, Christina Seder, Reginald Spivey, Jason Strader, Kim Wagner, and Michael Wladyka! Additionally, I want to thank two retirees, Richard Hill and Edna Suszko!

This book would not have been possible without everyone who contributed to the success of my company. I want to thank the first five investors who took the risk to provide the seed money to launch Thermagon: Delano Ingram, James Kirchner, Milan Busta, Richard Lancaster, and Martha Bates. My mentor and confidant, Paul Schlather, partner of Arthur Anderson first and later Price Waterhouse Coopers, connected me to the Cleveland business community, advised me on many corporate governance issues and provided countless financial recommendations. Charles Shaw, who was my first manufacturer's representative, connected me to Silicon Valley. Rakesh Bhatia, a thermal engineer at Intel, championed my products to a major design win at Intel Corporation. DJ Chou, my first Asian manufacturer's representative, connected me to business in Taiwan. James Smith and Woody Evans, my first employees worked initially for a mere $1,000 per month. To all of the employees who followed, your dedication to our business and sincere work ethic is much appreciated. Thank you!

Last but not least, my family played an incredible role in the success of Thermagon. When I quit my job and announced that I was going to start a business, the news was met with disbelief and concern. The first few years created an environment of insecurity for the entire family. I am sorry for your angst. Mom, as with most mothers, did her share of worrying. She helped me out wherever possible, lent me money early on to buy a much-needed piece of equipment, and was my guardian angel as I traveled the world, studying my itinerary and checking the weather conditions. Even though Dad was only present in spirit, I knew that he would be unbelievably proud of my accomplishment and would have been my right-hand man if he could have been with us.

My children were most affected by what appeared, at the time, to be a very foolhardy decision. Craig, my youngest, had just graduated from high school and was off to college. I had saved the money for his college education, but everyday living expenses were difficult to meet. When I leased my house and rented a condo forty miles away, attempting to live on the difference in rents, Craig felt totally displaced, as he did not have a real home to return to on college breaks. Thanks for making the most of a difficult situation, Craig! My daughter Diane was in California, insulated from the day-to-day problems of my starting a business. Jim, my oldest, had completed college and was having a successful experience with his first job. Not only was he able to manage on his own, but he was able to help me out on many occasions. I won't forget the time you hauled some cheap secondhand furniture for my plant in your truck. Susan, your then fiancée, came to work for me without pay. When Jim and Susan decided to get married, their wedding was in my home that I had returned to. We kept it simple and made it happen. Thank you for hanging in there with me in those early years. It wasn't until both Jim and Craig joined me at Thermagon that our progress developed. We all wore many hats and filled in for each other as needed. Together, we are the success of Thermagon. I humbly acknowledge and thank you for all you contributed.

PREFACE

We must make hay while the sun shines.
—Albert "Sunny" Hilkirk, dad

A s I have charged through life at a rather frantic pace, it never occurred to me to write a book about my entrepreneurial experience. Talking about myself makes me feel uncomfortable and the art of writing, as a scientist, seemed wrought with frustration and difficulty, but that all changed one beautiful evening in August 2016 when I crossed paths with a gentleman I'd never met before, a man who invited me to sit with him on a bench outside a music venue. "You must write your story down," he said.

Two and a half years later…and here you are inside the pages of my story. It makes one wonder if things don't happen for a reason and if the right people don't show up in your life (somehow) on purpose and at just the right time.

Being an avid music enthusiast, I attended a Cleveland Orchestra concert at Severance Hall. Seldom did they perform there in the summer months, so to encourage attendance, they hosted a cocktail party on the outdoor steps of the hall after the concert. As I was casually standing, enjoying the moment, a gentleman walked by and looked at me.

"Hi," I said.

With that simple hook, he stopped, and a conversation ensued. The rest is a bit of a blur. I only know from his reaction that I had quickly, spontaneously, and briefly told him about my entrepreneurial endeavor.

"Wait right there," he said. "I will be right back!"

I did what he asked. I waited. When he returned, he invited me to sit down with him on a nearby bench. I accepted but was beginning to become a bit nervous, not knowing what this was all about. As fate would have it, he wanted to learn more about my entrepreneurial experience. He responded so receptively and positively. That's when he told me that I needed to write down my story. I was stunned.

This gentleman was Joseph R. Degenfelder. Mr. Degenfelder, as I was about to learn, is an accomplished scientist, inventor, and businessman. He is also an avid supporter of the arts. Joseph is a 1961 chemical engineering graduate from Cornell University. He later continued his education with a master's degree in business administration from Weatherhead School of Management at Case Western Reserve University.

As an ordnance officer in the First Armored Division, he was on the advance party for the invasion of Cuba in the Russian Missile Crisis. Joseph, through his chemical engineering training, became an expert in the production and stabilization of polyvinyl chloride and polypropylene and in-plant design for chemicals such as alpha interferon and alternate fuel production. His work provided him the opportunity to travel the globe. Through these travels, Joseph and his wife, Pauline, have assembled a tremendous art collection, including Chinese jade, silk-scroll paintings, Imari porcelain, minerals, and Victor Vasarely optical art.

In my mind, bumping into this man was kismet. I have come to believe that Joseph's outstanding successes and accomplishments throughout his life came not only from his education, his intelligence, his creativity, and his hard work but also from his keen interest and curiosity about the people he has encountered in this life, resulting in a network of connections of infinite value.

So the fact that Joseph took an interest in me and took the time to listen to my entrepreneurial story all but convinced me that there was value in documenting my experience.

One day, soon after that day on the bench with Joseph, I said to myself, "Okay, maybe I can do this!" And so I opened my computer and began to write. The writing process was slow and arduous but extremely cathartic and rewarding. Thank you, Joseph, for launching me on this journey!

Journey toward Becoming an Entrepreneur

CHAPTER ONE

THE FORMATIVE YEARS

*Always treasure family and show compassion
and respect for all their endeavors.*

Unlike today, as I grew up in the forties and fifties, the word entrepreneur was seldom heard or used and was one that I don't recall identifying with. Today the word entrepreneur has become a buzzword, used to label almost anyone who has experienced success in business. Schools, colleges, and universities provide studies and courses in entrepreneurship. This begs the question, "Can entrepreneurship truly be taught, or is it the culmination of inherited traits and experiences focused sharply toward the endeavor of creating or developing a successful business?"

The dictionary defines an entrepreneur as someone who organizes and manages a business, assuming the risk for the sake of profit. I always put the most emphasis on the ability to assume risk. So as I started down this path of creating a business, I developed my own definition of an entrepreneur—someone who can successfully create a business starting with, what I refer to as, the "five nos"—no products, no physical facility, no employees, no customers, and no money.

So here begins the story of my journey to successful entrepreneurship. As a child, I can recall the makeshift desk that I cherished in a low-ceilinged room where I imagined I was running a factory. I always liked to make things and became an accomplished seamstress at a young age. I would define my childhood and youth as quite normal and nurturing. My upbringing was very middle class in Sharon, a small industrial town in Western Pennsylvania. Neither of my parents had the opportunity to attend college although they were quite intelligent in their own right. Many times in my life, I was asked if my parents were entrepreneurs. Dad, who was very analytical and had a photographic memory, was very traditional and conservative, yet certainly not an entrepreneur. Rather, he spent his whole career in the corporate world with one company.

He began his career during the Great Depression at Westinghouse Corporation in his teens. In order to get a machinist position, he pretended to be older and misrepresented his age. Then he became a draftsman on his ascent to management, where he led a division in large transformer manufacturing. Dad seldom talked about his work at home, so details of his experience are sketchy. Maybe that is why I seldom brought my work home, so not to interfere with my personal life and my family.

On the other hand, there was a spark of entrepreneurship in my mother, who talked about her beautician business that she had before my sister and I were born. In those days, almost all married women with children ultimately made their career as a full-time homemaker and mother. Of my parents, my mother was definitely the risk-taker. I have never forgotten the day that she told me "I'm no Goody Two-shoes." As I grew up, my parents encouraged a life that valued honesty, hard work, and trust. Those traits have served me well on my journey to becoming an entrepreneur.

Looking back, I think certain entrepreneurial traits must have been part of my DNA from the beginning. One great example of this was when I decided on my own in the seventh grade that I wanted to play a musical instrument. I wandered into the school music room and asked what instruments they had that I could learn to play. Two were available—a violin and a tenor saxophone.

At that stage in my life, I perceived violins to be high-pitched and squawky, so my decision to choose the saxophone was a no-brainer. After school, I returned to the music room to pick up the sax and carry it home. Not a bad idea, but I took public transportation to school and needed to transfer from one bus line to another. I also had a considerable walk on each end. In case you don't know the size of a tenor saxophone, I'm not sure which was bigger, the saxophone or me.

By the time I made my way home, I was pretty wiped out. Instead of going to the back door, which was my normal routine, I made it only as far as the front door and rang the bell. When my mother answered the door, I think she nearly fainted to see that I had dragged that large saxophone home all by myself.

If entrepreneurs need tenacity, then I think maybe I was blessed, as my parents surely helped facilitate that attribute in me. To demonstrate the kind of nurturing and support I received from my parents growing up, I think that was the last time I took the large instrument on the city bus. My mom always made sure she drove me on the days that I needed the saxophone. Many happy memories still exist from my experiences playing that tenor, woodwind instrument in the band, orchestra, and jazz band.

High school was about taking all the college preparatory classes available in the fifties. Science and mathematics were my favorites! I participated in nearly all the extracurricular activities offered. I knew from a very young age that college was in my future even though my parents had to live frugally in order to save sufficient money. I finished high school well within the top 10 percent, academically speaking. The big decision was where I would go to college and what I would study. Those questions loomed heavy on my mind. I had the grandiose idea that Duke University would be a great choice, but my parents had other ideas.

My sister had gone to Ohio Wesleyan University, and my parents fell in love with the place. I was accepted everywhere I applied. Ohio Wesleyan, however, was the only school that offered financial aid. Knowing that sending me to college was a financial sacrifice for my parents, I agreed to go to Ohio Wesleyan. I've never regretted that decision, and to this day, I am a very large proponent of a liberal arts education.

So what was I going to study? This was yet another big decision. After much soul-searching, I decided to pursue a degree in chemistry. In 1957, the year I graduated from high school, Russia launched

Sputnik, the first artificial earth satellite. With that came a large wave of emphasis toward studying science.

Life at Ohio Wesleyan was not easy for me. Being of average intelligence, it took considerable effort and hard work to master the tasks at hand, not only in science but also the liberal arts. Many hours were spent in labs, not only for my own courses but also for work as a lab assistant to support my financial aid. I joined a sorority and played in the band for a while, but little time was left for extracurricular activities. With many of my sorority sisters studying elementary education, taking courses they referred to as "kiddie's games" and "kiddie's literature," I often wondered why I found it so important to study chemistry. After all, at the end of the day, my sorority sisters would receive the same diploma as me, a bachelor of arts degree. I never seriously considered switching out of chemistry. One might ask, why not? Was it my innate tenacity or just plain old stubbornness? Would I ever understand why mastering those classes in chemistry, physics, calculus was so important? A bachelor of arts degree in chemistry is an oxymoron, one might say. Most scientists, even though they may have attended a liberal arts college, receive a bachelor's degree in science, not the arts. My perception is that science students with a bachelor of arts degree have been exposed to a far more diverse curriculum. I would often refer to my liberal arts education as the key to success in building a business on discoveries in science. My degree in liberal arts taught me how to approach and solve problems using critical thinking techniques, which were probably much more important than the skills I learned in chemistry. Together they made a dynamite combination and, I believe, were a critical component to my success as an entrepreneur.

After graduation, landing a job was my next order of business. Having skill in the sciences was a big plus. Also, between my junior and senior years at Ohio Wesleyan, I received a job for the summer at Eastman Kodak. Today that would be considered an internship, but back then, it was simply a summer job. My work ethic and attention to detail served me well. Kodak tried hard to convince me to return after graduation. However, I decided not to return to Eastman Kodak. Still, that experience helped me receive multiple job offers, and I, ultimately, chose a position with Standard Oil of Ohio, otherwise known as Sohio.

For the early sixties, Sohio seemed open to providing opportunities for women. Sohio gave me the choice of working either in the research center or the development center. I chose the latter despite the fact the research center was new and probably more appealing on the surface. Somehow, at this early stage of my career planning, I seemed to realize that for me developing things for real-world problems was more appealing than engaging in pure research in a field that seemed to me to have vague outcomes.

So off I went to Cleveland, Ohio, to begin my career at Sohio's Development Center in the industrial flats with a bird's-eye view of the oil refineries—closer to the action…or so I thought. I was ready to set the world on fire. I was ready to solve real-world problems rather than being a pure research chemist in search of basic knowledge. Simply put, I was an analytical chemistry technician.

First off, I needed to learn the tests and techniques for analyzing hydrocarbon products so that, hopefully, I would be given the opportunity to develop new techniques and tests for use in the refining process. I was probably overeager to learn, as well as needing to know the purpose of the tests and their importance in the process. I was quickly learning that I was not satisfied with performing tasks for the sake of reporting numbers, but rather I also needed to know their significance to the overall business for my own satisfaction. I was not a pure research person who was driven by the thrill of learning or discovering something new just for the sake of knowing or reporting but rather was a person more motivated by how information, new or reconfigured, could become useful in solving real-world problems.

Oh boy, was I naive! Sohio did not react positively to my many questions concerning the value and significance of the tests I was completing. No one appeared to work very hard nor have much enthusiasm for the work at hand. I was quickly learning that the majority of the employees were there for the paycheck at day's end, and the work was merely a routine process.

One example of the Sohio culture was supervision's attitude toward the resignation of a young engineer who was known for being quite brilliant. I am talking the upper fifth of the upper fifth in intelligence. Sohio management didn't understand how to challenge him, which was made obvious by their comments that "they hoped his new employer understood who they were hiring."

Nonetheless, my overall day-to-day experience at Sohio was quite pleasant. I am quite gregarious, and I soon made many friends with whom I socialized. My friends became an important piece of my life. This was quite important since I had come to Cleveland alone and was making my way independently. And professionally speaking, I was feeling frustrated with both the significance and the impact of the work that I was producing.

Typical of what many young women do in their early twenties, I married a gentleman introduced to me by one of my Sohio friends. A year later, I became pregnant and soon learned that at seven months, I would be escorted out the door. My career was over! In 1960, the world of American women was limited in almost every respect, from family life to the work life. A woman was expected to follow one path: marry in her early twenties, quickly start a family, and devote the rest of her life to homemaking.

Women had limited legal rights to their husbands' property and earnings, and divorce was very difficult. The 38 percent of women who worked in 1960 were largely limited to jobs in the fields of teaching, nursing, and secretarial work. Women were generally not welcome in professional programs and, as a result, accounted for 6 percent of American doctors, 3 percent of lawyers, and less than 1 percent of engineers. Despite this dismal picture, in 1961, when I launched my career, Sohio was very progressive in their attitude toward women employees for the time.

They recruited women for their R&D programs and paid what I believed to be a fair wage. My salary of $7,200 per year gave me bragging rights among my fellow women workers. I am not certain whether or not men hired for similar jobs at Sohio were receiving higher salaries. However, I do recall that companies, including Sohio, did not offer paid pregnancy leaves or short-term disability. Of all the women I knew within this organization, nearly 100 percent of them did not have children.

Since day-care facilities were not available, unless you had a family to take care of your children or you could afford a nanny, full-time working careers were not an option. And, in those days, it was expected that at seven months into a pregnancy, a woman was forced to leave her job. It was not a leave-of-absence but rather a termination of employment and, quite possibly, the abrupt end to a budding career.

The birth of one's first child is probably one of the most life-changing events that one will experience. Suffering from a bad case of "cabin fever" and some form of homesickness, I began the role of the full-time mother. Soon my love of that child and its need for constant care encompassed me, and I knew that I could not return to work anytime soon. And so for the next eighteen years, I was a full-time homemaker and, ultimately, the mother of three children. Believe it or not, I do not regret one minute of it. This was truly my most difficult role. From a nurturer to a mediator, to an educator, to a cheerleader—one's ability to adapt in order to solve real-world problems were in play each and every day.

Overall, I learned how to inspire people to perform certain functions without the use of any materialistic or monetary reward. I began volunteering, and my work as a volunteer during those years became a very valuable experience. I learned that treating people as human beings rather than as mere names on a roster would reap many rewards. I now know that these experiences provided valuable preparation toward my success as an entrepreneur.

CHAPTER TWO

RETURN TO THE WORKFORCE

*Success comes from venturing
out of your comfort zone.*

In 1981, after eighteen years of marriage, I found myself divorced with three children, ages ten, fifteen, and seventeen. Divorce is not for the faint of heart. I took my marriage vows seriously, yet I became increasingly unhappy and dissatisfied with my life. My husband became increasingly dysfunctional with the birth of each child to the point that his dependency on me became a burden rather than a help in fostering our children. I paced, hours on end, trying to determine whether a continuation of my current plight or a life as a single parent would be more manageable. One thing is for sure, neither choice was going to be easy.

When life got to the point where my husband's presence in the home became more than just a burden but also a detriment to the children, I decided to act. I chose to start a new life. I realized that he had become an alcoholic. I must admit that this is one of the saddest moments in my life. Mine was one of the few divorces that occurred without any third-party interference.

The world was rebounding from the oil crisis of the seventies and the Jimmy Carter years, an era of extremely high-interest rates. In search of a job, I reached out to Sohio who was experiencing much success with its exploration of Prudhoe Bay and the Alaskan Pipeline. Hoping that my Sohio development work from the sixties might open the door for a new job opportunity, I was able to land a temporary position in alternate energy research. The next eight years were exceedingly difficult and life changing as I plodded my way from a part-time job as a lab assistant in alternate energy to the founder of a company called Thermagon.

Little did I know that the events of the eighties would play a significant role in my journey. British Petroleum (BP) acquired controlling interest of Sohio. Apple and IBM released their first personal computers. An oil glut was in the making, causing a decline in oil prices, and Sohio purchased Kennecott, a major copper producer. With Kennecott, came two of its subsidiaries, Carborundum Company and Dorr-Oliver. These events were reason for constant change at Sohio/BP.

I believe the ability to react and embrace change may be the key to many positive outcomes! I survived the first year as a part-time employee, mainly because it gave me some extra time to attend to some personal issues. However, professionally speaking, I needed to be there every day in order to play a significant role and advance my skills.

Working with computers was new to me, as it was to many of the other employees, so I was able to learn along with them. By the second year, I was hired full time as a laboratory technician in alternate energy. Sohio was busy hiring many new young PhDs. So it wasn't long until I was given the opportunity to work with one of these new hires. Until then, I had been performing rather routine and menial tasks to improve catalysts that would hopefully be used to convert the tailings, or the black crap, as I called it, to something useful.

The oil-refining process takes petroleum, a rather thick black liquid, from the ground and refines it into gasoline and many other clear liquids of commercial value via a distillation process. During this process, the petroleum gets separated into liquid fractions according to their boiling points. What is left is a very thick black liquid, often called tailings, that oil companies want to convert into a commercial product.

I was very happy to have this new hire become my new immediate supervisor. We hit it off immediately. We were both high energy with the technical skills and the means to implement the ideas in an efficient and practical way. We made a very effective team. We succeeded on projects like converting methanol to diesel fuel and cracking methane to a greater than 95 percent stream of hydrogen.

The energy crisis of the seventies was a period when the major industrial countries of the world faced substantial oil shortages, real and perceived, as well as elevated prices. These major industrial centers were forced to contend with escalating issues related to oil supply. Western countries were forced to rely on potentially unfriendly countries, such as in the Middle East, for their oil resources. In 1980, following the Iraqi invasion of Iran, the Iranian oil production nearly stopped, and the Iraqi oil supply declined as well. The resulting high oil prices led to slowed economic activity and energy conservation. In addition, oil companies were looking for alternative energy sources that resulted in projects like mine to convert methanol, a non-oil-related material, into a diesel fuel.

Sohio was generally late to the party and did not decide to explore these alternative fuel ideas until the mideighties. Oil prices peaked in 1980 and started a decline thereafter, resulting in an oil glut. In 1986, oil prices crashed, probably causing Sohio's lack of interest in our successful results in producing diesel fuel from methanol.

With the oil glut of the eighties, BP's oil wells in Alaska and in Texas were adding to the surplus. Methane was being flared or burned off the wells with little regard for its value. And so my project for converting methane into hydrogen was born. The thought was that pure hydrogen would be more valuable than the methane.

Success, here again, fell on deaf ears.

At Sohio, success on your project was a means for reassignment to another project rather than being encouraged to further develop the successful findings. Management was not capable of making decisions on how to move our work forward toward commercialization. The timeliness or relevance of projects was not often obvious to those of us doing the research.

In retrospect, management's ability to select appropriate projects in a timely manner seemed suspect and created an atmosphere of useless endeavor. Employees were evaluated on how many laboratory notebooks were filled and on how many submissions were made of inventors' disclosure forms, documents written by a scientist or an engineer to help a company's patent department or a patent attorney determine whether patent protection should be sought for the invention. The potential usefulness or real-world application of the work never seemed to be considered. To me, it seemed like there was no possible path through the maze to get to the end goal of building a successful product or career.

CHAPTER THREE

SABOTAGE IN THE SCIENCE LAB

You need the tenacity of a pit bull.

Sabotage can be defined as the intentional and deliberate obstruction of, or damage to any cause, movement, activity, or effort. For me, the thought that I personally could become a victim of sabotage seemed impossible. However, in a corporate environment where success is vaguely defined, marginally attainable; and where management is weak, insecure, and condescending, the probability of one's work, being sabotaged could conceivably increase from the perceived zero.

My difficulties began with somewhat minor harassment issues, such as corporate mail being detained or misplaced. Then one day, my personal calculator had several keys that began to stick.

Hmmm…

All the laboratories were stocked with squirt bottles filled with acetone for cleaning glassware. In our business, it was common knowledge that spraying acetone on plastic would partially dissolve it and make it sticky.

Had my calculator been sprayed with acetone?

An accident? One would hope!

When this happened a second time, I began to wonder. During the time of the "Methanol to Diesel" project, we used a calculating integrator to compute our data. There were several mornings I would come into the laboratory to find that the keys had been squirted with acetone and were stuck together. This meant stopping all work, ordering a new integrator, and waiting until it arrived to resume work on the project. No one ever questioned the expense of replacing the integrators. It was now becoming obvious that someone was intentionally causing destruction and detaining work on the project. It was becoming obvious that the perpetrator was my supervisor. My coworker and I carried on despite the aggravations without reporting the episodes to management. At least no one's life was put in danger.

During the time of my project to convert methanol to a greater than 95 percent stream of hydrogen, these acts of sabotage started to escalate. In the simplest of terms, I was cracking methane (CH_4) into hydrogen (H_2) at very high temperatures and leaving Carbon (C) behind on the catalyst. Once the catalyst became loaded with carbon, the reaction no longer worked. The second part of the process, also at high temperature, was to use oxygen to make carbon monoxide and carbon dioxide to remove the carbon from the catalyst, thus to revive the catalyst and to once again make hydrogen. This was called a "two-cycle process." You may have figured out by now that my reactor was plumbed with both methane and oxygen. The valves to control these gases into the reactor were laboratory style and easy to turn on and off. As I carried out the reactions, I took samples of the gases coming from my reactor about every ten minutes and analyzed their content. That way, I knew whether or not I was getting an adequate supply of hydrogen, and whether or not I was successfully removing the carbon from the catalyst.

One day, the unthinkable happened. As I was making hydrogen in my high-temperature reactor, the gas analysis of my product contained oxygen. Could it be true? Had someone flipped the valve and put oxygen into my reactor? No other explanation seemed feasible. I immediately turned off all gases and heat and went straight to my coworker with the analytical proof of what had just happened. We all know that hydrogen, when exposed to oxygen, will explode. Why my reaction did not explode, I will never know. Any mishap with my reaction would have been considered my fault. Had it exploded and I lived to tell about it, I would have certainly lost my job. At this juncture, I went to management and reported what had happened, to which they responded, "You need to watch your experiments and equipment more closely."

Really?

I was shocked and appalled by their apathy and by their inaction but mostly by their complicity in this increasingly dangerous situation. To remain obedient and to hopefully prevent further sabotage, I turned my desk (one of three in an office meant for one) around to face the door. This way, I could see my reactor at most times. I also drilled holes in the valve handles that controlled the intake of gases to my reactor, threading wire through the holes and wiring the valves to the pipes so that no one could easily turn the valve handles. Hopefully, that would deter anyone from mixing oxygen into my reactor while I was generating hydrogen. Apparently, my supervisor was upset that the catalyst that he had developed was not being used in this process. The reason being, it did not work for this reaction.

I felt certain that my catalyst would be contaminated next. My only recourse was to turn off my high-temperature reactor midafternoon, cool it to room temperature, pour the catalyst out into a jar, put it into my purse, and take it home with me. I had no choice but to protect myself and my work as best I could since I knew I couldn't count on the support of the British Petroleum management team. They gave me no concern and, in reality, gave me no credibility. I was beginning to wonder how long could I endure this type of work environment?

CHAPTER FOUR

A CLEAN SHEET OF PAPER

> Real innovation comes from starting with a clean slate, resisting the temptation to simply tweak what already exists.

As determined as I am, I endured several years of this unhealthy work environment until, fortunately, I was given the opportunity to become part of an "idea development team." This team was charged with the task of solving industrial problems occurring at Dorr-Oliver and Carborundum, both subsidiaries acquired when Sohio purchased Kennicott. Dorr-Oliver makes large separation equipment for chemical processing, and Carborundum is a ceramics and composite company dating back to the 1890s.

Ceramics are inorganic, nonmetallic materials, usually crystalline oxides, nitrides, or carbides. Carborundum was known mainly for their silicon carbide, boron nitride, and aluminum nitride, supplying abrasive, refractory, and insulation products to a wide variety of industries such as steel, automotive, space exploration, and electronics. I was involved in solving a scale problem with Dorr-Oliver equipment occurring in the Bayer Process for converting bauxite to aluminum oxide and, ultimately, reducing it to aluminum. Through Carborundum, I became involved in electronic materials, developing dopants for silicon chips, and metallizing aluminum nitride substrates. Each new project meant starting over on the learning curve in that industry, a very laborious and time-consuming endeavor.

I learned at my new position that heat was quickly becoming a huge issue in electronic systems as they decreased in size and increased in functionality and speed. Carborundum was working feverishly on aluminum nitride for high thermal conductivity substrates for the electronics industry, and much energy and expertise was being focused there. Electronics are based on the integrated circuit, an assembly of millions of interconnected components such as transistors and resistors that are all built up on a tiny chip of silicon. In order to maintain their reliability, these circuits depend on insulating materials that can serve as substrates (that is the bases on which the microscopic electronic components and their connections are built) and packages (that is the structures that seal a circuit from the environment and make it a single compact unit.)

Ceramics are known for having good electrical insulating properties and have found applications for these substrates and packages. Alumina was the mostly commonly used material for these applications. Carborundum was attempting to take this technology a step further and develop aluminum nitride substrates because of their high thermal conductivity.

My idea was to make polymers thermally conductive and electrically insulating as a means to fill the air gap between the hard surfaces (ceramics or metal) of an electronic system. If the heat generated by the chips was not moved out and away to ambient air, the system was sure to fail.

My proposal to develop these materials "fell between the cracks," as I was told by BP managers for many weeks. Despite the initial resistance to my proposal, I was ultimately able to get approval for a project to develop thermally conductive polymers.

My plan of attack to make polymer systems that were both thermally conductive and electrically insulating used boron nitride powder manufactured by Carborundum. It was used as a filler in polymer systems that were soft and flexible. I combed the literature and learned that researchers found little success in achieving high thermal conductivity with ceramic-filled polymers.

That said, I believe that to truly discover something unique and revolutionary, one must start with a clean piece of paper. Modifying something that already exists will rarely lead to significant results. Intuitively, I thought about how best to combine ceramic powders (especially boron nitride) with a polymer so as to not totally destroy the thermal properties of the ceramic itself. It was not long before I received unexpected results: values for thermal conductivity greater than ten times any found in the literature.

This was definitely one of those "aha" moments!

I tried other ceramic powders as well as boron nitride. I came to believe that it was the friable, easily broken platelets of boron nitride that, with careful handling, could produce interesting materials. The process was designed to generate as little shear as possible so as not to break up the platelets.

Commercially available ceramic/polymer products used common alumina (aluminum oxide) as fillers and a solvent-based process that produced very low thermally conductive materials. Alumina, a powder with small hard particles, was mixed into a polymer that had been dissolved in a solvent. The mixture was then coated on a fiberglass cloth, and the solvent evaporated off. The evaporated solvent went into the atmosphere as a pollutant. Unfortunately, or fortunately, depending how you look at it, BP showed little interest and thought the work had little value.

The process I developed relied 100 percent on solids, meaning there was no need to use solvents and was totally "green." The green process meant that the materials were manufactured without admitting any contaminants into the atmosphere. My process used a proprietary mixing procedure to combine the filler material with the polymer directly without the use of solvents. The resulting mixture was then formed into sheets of a specified thickness using custom-made equipment. No toxic or unwanted byproducts were generated during this process.

The world was just beginning to recognize the ill effects of many industrial processes that emitted toxic chemicals into the atmosphere. Therefore, little attention or recognition for our "green" process was forthcoming, much different from the recognition one would receive in today's world.

In my effort to be a good corporate citizen, I decided to file for a patent on my findings. This was my first attempt at filing. I understood that any patents granted while working at a corporation belonged to the corporation, itself, not to the inventor. My strategy was to devise a formula that could define the specific particle size distribution range of a ceramic powder that would provide high thermal conductivity when combined with a polymer matrix. Most other parameters specified were quite obvious, such as purity and particle shape. Anyone trying to understand how I could achieve such high thermal conductivity numbers could analyze the composite and immediately know that the filler was boron nitride. The patent application was filed in March of 1989. I had little expectation that the patent would ever be granted. However, in the event that the patent was granted, British Petroleum would become its sole owner. All rights of pursuing or protecting the patent would belong to them.

Meanwhile, the events of the past several years at British Petroleum were beginning to wear me down. At one point, when it was time for my evaluation, my supervisor, instead of giving me the grade that he admitted I deserved, he placed a minus sign in front of the number to block my possibility of getting a raise. He claimed that he was instructed by his supervisors to not allow anyone to get a pay raise. To that explanation, I expounded with a pound on the desk and declared, "That's bullshit! Please just put a zero on the paper. This has no meaning." He was irked by my response but refused to put a zero on my evaluation. He knew I was right.

I was becoming more and more determined to make a marketing success of my technology for making polymers thermally conductive. Starting over again on a new technology was not an option that I thought I could face one more time. I began to fantasize about how I could take this technology to market on my own. That "fantasy" provoked a deeper hope in me that, perhaps, one day, I could detect a very slight crack in Sohio/BP's back door through which I could quietly slip.

CHAPTER FIVE

A CRACK IN THE DOOR

Don't just do what you love. Chase what makes
you curious.

—Jeff Goins, author

So many questions started jumping around in my head, but the question that kept me up at night was this: "If the patent were to be granted, along with all of the data I had generated, would British Petroleum be able to claim ownership of what I hold in my brain?"

I noodled with a friend on what to name my company if I started my own venture. We thought the name Thermagon would be most fitting. Thermagon, meaning, "heat be gone." With each passing day, I became more determined to find a way to make a success of this technology. Suddenly, two roads had diverged before me: one path meant a life career at BP, a life in which I relied on faith that they would support my efforts. The second, unknown path, was to leave BP and attempt to start my own business. Neither option at first glance had a very high probability for success. This fork in the road was a significant juncture for me. At that point, I wasn't sure what to do, but fate stepped in.

Later in 1989, BP was planning an electronic design center in Phoenix and considered pursuing my work there. They asked me to visit this center, which was in the initial stages of development. This provided me with a perfect opportunity to test their level of interest in pursuing this technology I had become so passionate about. I arrived with a simple business plan that my friend and I had put together. I had questions that needed to be answered.

Yes, it was unusual, at least in the BP culture, for someone like me to be so forthright as to test the sincerity of their employer and their employer's interest in their work. However, at this point, I had made a commitment to myself to take one of two roads, and as I was already at BP, I wanted to make sure I wasn't leaving a worthwhile opportunity behind.

When I arrived at the Carborundum/BP facility in Phoenix, the people managing the design center made no effort to schedule time to discuss my project or even the possibility that I would move to Phoenix to pursue my work there. Instead, they sent me out with a real estate agent to find a house.

In no way had I given them the impression that I had agreed to move there! I was annoyed that my time was being wasted. I immediately proceeded to schedule my return trip to Cleveland. Before my cab arrived to take me to the airport, the project leader arrived in my hotel room for a meeting.

If this sounds strange, it was!

I had had business meetings in hotel lobbies before but never in my hotel room. Of course, I had no witnesses, so there was no point reporting the incident. Our discussion was useless. It became obvious that little to no thought had been placed on a plan to develop my technology.

I asked many questions: If I were to move to this new facility in Phoenix, what would my role be? What would my salary be? How much money and human resources would they invest in the success of my project? To which they had zero answers.

They made it clear that I was out of line to even suggest they might have answers to these questions. Needless to say, no agreement was reached in Phoenix. At that point, I was in trouble with the BP research bigwigs in Cleveland. My need for answers was viewed as insubordination, and so I was called into a meeting with my immediate supervisor and the department manager. Of course, he made sure he had a witness. They proceeded to tell me that I would be removed from the project and "Blah, blah, blah!"

I kept silent.

When there was finally a lull in the conversation, I stood up and politely asked to be excused. To which the department manager pointed his finger at me and screamed, "No! Sit down!" At that moment, I knew it was over with me and BP. I refused to be treated with such disrespect in both Phoenix and Cleveland. However, I did as he asked. I sat down, but for the remainder of the meeting, I stared blankly out the window, knowing that I would be leaving very soon.

I believed that I had an idea. This idea, if developed into products, would be a breakthrough in the thermal management of electronics. If I stayed at BP/Sohio research, there was no possible way I'd be able to create a successful product or bring it to market. The culture was degrading and defeating and without purpose or meaning. Employees were only meant to satisfy the whims of their immediate supervisor. I needed more. I needed to solve real-world problems, not pander the powers that be. The truth be known, I never had a boss that I respected. By my definition, a boss is meant to represent his direct reports within the company. That never happened in my experiences with BP.

Within the next day or so, in the latter part of 1989, I turned in my resignation. This time, I was prepared for negative feedback; I had a tape recorder hidden in my pocket. Before the end of the day, my supervisor came to me with an offer of a grade-level promotion and an increase in pay, to which I responded, "Too little, too late."

Despite the apparent spontaneity of my departure, I had quietly and carefully planned my exit. Thankfully, over the years, I had used BP's resources to learn as much as possible. I certainly learned what not to do when managing a company. BP continued their vindictive behavior by trying to withhold my last paycheck and canceling my health insurance through COBRA. Both acts were grounds for a lawsuit. For all I cared, I was now free to take my gained knowledge and character-building experiences with me to create a company named Thermagon. Incidentally, twelve years down the road, on October 30, 2001, *Inc. Magazine* would write an article about my departure from BP, titled "You Had Your Chance" by Susan Hansen. The subtitle read: "Some of the Best Ideas Are Those Offered by Employees to Employers. And Some of the Best Companies Are Born When Those Employers Say No."

The year 1989 was often referred to as the "Year of Hopes." Many believed that a dark chapter in history had ended and that the road to a happier future lay clear ahead as described by Margaret MacMillan in the final edition of the *Wall Street Journal* of 2018. Visions of the Germans drinking champagne on the top of the Berlin Wall as it was coming down. China's vicious response to the protests of Tiananmen Square in Beijing seemed to put them on the wrong side of history. The peaceful dissolution of the Soviet Union seemed to indicate that real democracy could win out all over the world. The great powerful countries of the world would no longer need vast arsenals of destructive weapons. Just two years before, in 1987, President Reagan and Soviet leader Mikhail Gorbachev signed an agreement that barred the possession, production, and flight testing of United States and Russian ground launched ballistic and cruise missiles with ranges between 300 miles and 3,400 miles. Yes, indeed, 1989 was a time of great hope, not only for me and my business venture but also for the world over!

Taking a Leap of Faith

The Pre-Start-Up Phase of Thermagon

C H A P T E R   S I X

SETTING THE STAGE

Stay abreast of what's relevant in the world.

The next two to three years, following my departure from Sohio/BP, I call the pre-start-up phase of Thermagon. To better understand the timeliness of the objective of Thermagon, which is to provide the world of electronics with thermal conducting materials significantly better than those currently available, putting my work into context within several events of the eighties would be helpful.

I was convinced that heat was certain to be a huge problem for electronics as size continued to decrease and performance and functionality increased. However, I was too consumed in the nitty-gritty of BP to take note of the details of some significant happenings of the eighties. Entrepreneurs Steve Jobs and Steve Wozniak took Apple, their small computer company, public with an IPO in 1980. They quickly built up their customer base to 250,000 customers with 1,000 dealers across the world with their Apple I, Apple II, and Apple III models.

It was the Apple III that Jobs declared would not have a cooling fan but rather would take the heat out by conduction through the chassis. His methods did not work, and the model failed miserably. This is one of the few references of a company acknowledging a "heat" problem.

In 1981, IBM introduced the IBM personal computer with one model, 200 dealers, no databases, and one-word-processing program.

Apple was very arrogant and neglected to heed the developments of IBM. By 1983, the IBM PC surpassed the Apple II, and by 1984 had $4 billion in revenue, twice that of Apple's, and a market share of 56 percent of American companies as customers versus Apple's 16 percent market share.

In 1983, Apple completed development of the Macintosh, a 128k computer. In January 1984, Apple introduced it to the world through the famous television commercial at Super Bowl XVIII. The initial sales and excitement soon slowed, and the product success began to decline. This led to disagreement in strategy between John Sculley, Apple's CEO at the time, and Steve Jobs. In 1985, Jobs left Apple, and during his absence, the company nearly folded. Eventually, in 1997, Jobs returned to lead Apple, saving it from its bland personal computer offerings and a stale operating system.

That said, Apple was not a major player in the nineties as it pertained to the growth of Thermagon. It was market leaders like IBM, Dell, Compaq, and others driven by the Intel microprocessors that drove the Thermagon business. It wasn't until the turn of the century that Apple appeared on our radar screen and became a customer. Other electronic advances of the eighties included Walkman, VCRs, camcorders, and video game consoles. In order to meet the growing demand of these many new advances, there were issues that needed to be addressed.

CHAPTER SEVEN

AVOIDING COURT

Never sue or be sued.

Silently, I pretended to have no concern of a threat from BP. The truth be known, I was terrified that they would use their deep pockets and their vindictive nature to come after me. Their interest in my work always seemed superficial. Consequently, I was very cautious about sharing in-depth discussions with them on the "art of the process" that influenced the material's properties. I believed, from the bottom of my heart, that BP could not make a success of the technology that I left behind for them.

Could they take ownership of what was in my head? Who knows? Their electronic design center in Phoenix did not have positive outcomes. How vindictive could they be? With their deep pockets, would they choose to sue me? I had discussed the injustices of my BP experience with several fellow BP employees, some of whom had sued them with a positive outcome. If misery loves company, there were other disgruntled BP employees to lean on. As a result, I found an attorney who was willing to take my case, based on his success against BP on other similar matters. I filed a complaint with the Equal Employment Opportunity Commission (EEOC.) The truth be known, I had no interest in suing BP and was hopeful that I would not be involved with a lawsuit of any kind. How counter-productive would that be? This was an defensive move, something to give the company pause before coming for me. I never withdrew my complaint from the EEOC. I simply let the statutes of limitation run out. Whether this acted as a deterrent for BP, keeping them from suing me, I'll never know. It was always my hope that BP would find bigger problems to solve than to pursue a lawsuit against me.

In these early days of the pre-start-up phase, I chose to keep a very low profile. I turned down opportunities to publish papers and any other promotional materials. It was in July of 1991 that *Surface Mount Technology* finally published the paper that I had been asking them to hold off on for many months. This published paper precipitated a letter response from BP. The letter was not sent certified, so I immediately deposited it in the "circular file," never to be seen or heard from again. One would think that BP had more important issues to face than going after a technology they didn't understand, had little interest in, and had zero fit with their core business.

There was one other issue concerning BP that was lurking in my mind. That was how to purchase boron nitride from Carborundum, a company that was still a subsidiary of BP. The solution was to purchase the boron nitride through a friend, a company called Techways. That way, it was not directly tied to Thermagon. That worked very well until our volumes went up, and they became curious and wanted to visit us. The Carborundum people started following us around to trade shows. We avoided a visit as long as we could. Now it was clear my work could offer a positive result for the boron nitride business of Carborundum. And, as luck would have it, the threat completely went away when BP sold Carborundum to Saint-Gobain in February of 1995.

With all that in mind, would I recommend others quit their job and start a company based on a technology developed at their former employer? Probably not!

My decision was based on

1. the difficult work environment I endured;
2. my in-depth understanding of the BP players and their entrepreneurial ineptness; and
3. my desperate need to find another career path where I had a chance to succeed.

Being an entrepreneur is not for the faint of heart. Such a life-changing decision depends on your appetite for risk. Interference from BP would probably have ended my launch of Thermagon and, consequently, sent me into some other unknown venture. My advice in such a situation is this: know the facts, understand your appetite for risk, and prepare for the worst of outcomes. If you make the plunge, put your head down, stay focused on your goal, and make it happen and always maintain a sense of urgency!

During the pre-start-up phase of Thermagon, there was one other important issue that needed solving. How was I to protect my proprietary technology? There truly was no money for patents, and if I found a way, how would I protect them? In reality, the proprietary part of the product was in the processing secrets and the forms of the ingredients rather than on its composition. The products could not be reverse engineered, meaning, that analysis would not reveal the secret to their high thermal conductivity. The composition of the products could be determined by analysis. The processing techniques determined the outstanding properties and high thermal conductivity.

If I were to reveal these techniques in a patent, it would be nearly impossible to protect, even with money. The conclusion was to operate the company with trade secrets. "Trade secret" is defined as information used by a business, which can be legally protected that is secret to the general public and is critical to the livelihood and success of the business. How a product is made or ingredients that go into it, even customer lists, can be protected as a trade secret. Source codes for computer programs and the formula for Coca-Cola are common examples. The critical requirement for trade secret protection lies in maintaining the secret. Methods or information revealed to the public cannot be protected under trade secret laws. Therefore, no one was allowed in our factory except for the employees who, as you will learn, were incredibly loyal. They also signed nondisclosure agreements in order to become employees. Customers and suppliers were not allowed entry to our production area. This was critical since our process was the trade secret that we needed to protect. To enter a discussion with us or see our testing laboratory required signing a nondisclosure agreement. I realized that in order to have proprietary protection through trade secrets, I needed to be able to demonstrate that I had made a very conscientious effort to protect it. Please be aware that patents often provide a false sense of security. Securing a patent is no guarantee of business success.

Like most budding entrepreneurs trying to start a business, I seriously considered the possibility of having a partner. Having been active in the tennis community my whole life, I was learning that my fellow tennis players had varied professional skills that could be helpful at minimal cost. There was an attorney who I could bounce legal issues off; a printer who could provide letterhead paper; and an accountant who could help with financial statements, projections, taxes, etc. This accountant became my official accountant for Thermagon for many years. He also invested in the company. In addition to these finds was an electrical engineer who was unemployed. It seemed obvious to me that his technical skills could certainly be helpful in product design and application engineering. I was learning that many of the design engineers in the electronic industry were electrical engineers. So he offered to help with designing in the Thermagon products. I made him a partner. Unfortunately, it did not take more than a few months for me to realize that this guy had a corporate mentality. He was very theoretical, not very entrepreneurial-minded, and had little business sense. What a mess I had created! I conferred with one of my early investors and my attorney from the private placement memorandum, seeking help to dissolve this relationship. I was fortunate in that I was able to terminate our agreement with little consequence. Acting quickly was the secret to success.

In more recent years, I've encountered many businesspeople who became saddled with business partners that did not work out. Separating from a partner can be emotionally upsetting, not to mention costly. I would advise against partnering with anyone. My observations and experience have shown that it is only a matter of time before the partnership needs to be dissolved. Sharing equally seldom works. One person evolves as the leader and needs to have control. If you deem it essential to have a partner, make sure you have an attorney prepare very specific legal documents defining each of your roles and the procedure for separation.

CHAPTER EIGHT

SURVIVAL WITH NO INCOME

Start drinking poor man's coffee.

Soon I realized that having no income was not a laughing matter. How would I know that this venture may not work out? My children were now aged eighteen, twenty-three, and twenty-five, and I myself was the ripe old age of fifty. My children were speechless and scratching their heads on this latest development. My eldest, Jim, was graduated from college with a mechanical engineering degree and had an interesting job. My middle child, Diane, was nearly finished with college.

The good news is that I had saved money for each of their college educations, had a roof over my head in a house that was entirely paid for, and had no debt. But the reality of my situation was that my lifestyle, set in a rather high-end neighborhood, could no longer be maintained. I had some modest savings and investments that would hopefully keep me going me until I could generate revenue. The clock was ticking in my head. How long could I survive? I was not sure.

How was I to start a business in survival mode? The reality was that I had no products, no customers, no employees, no plant or facility, and no money. This led me to create my own definition of an entrepreneur to be someone who could successfully start a business with these "five nos." The real question was, what did I have that could give me a fighting chance?

First, I believed that I had a technology that could be developed into a family of thermally conductive products that would outperform anything in the marketplace by an order of magnitude. I believed that the electronics industry and computers, in particular, would desperately need these products to prevent their systems from catastrophic failure. Remember, as computing became faster, more functional and smaller, the heat created within the system became exponentially higher. Claims were that for every degree increase in the temperature of the chip, the failure rate would at least double.

Lastly, I believed that someone, somewhere, would understand my technology, and they would back me financially. This became my value proposition, providing high thermally conductive materials so that the electronics industry had a path forward without failures caused by overheating.

My head was down, and I was focused. By January of 1990, I had completed a proper business plan. In my day, a business plan was a formal written document beginning with an executive summary. The detailed plan to follow included a company analysis, industry analysis, market analysis, and a financial analysis. The document was marked confidential and distributed to a select group of people who were deemed to be potential investors. A pitch deck was unheard of. In today's world, a pitch deck is a PowerPoint presentation that serves as a promotional tool, sometimes used in place of a formal business plan but lacking in-depth analysis.

My naivete and optimism led me to believe that once a potential investor heard my story, they would be eager to invest. I was starting to learn that a continuing knowledge in the following areas would be imperative to success: state of the United States and global economy, availability of money, state-of-the-art technology, my market industries, raw material availability, and competitors. The decision of whether to finance the company through debt or equity became crucial. Feeling quite certain that banks would never take the risk of a loan, certainly not without attaching my only asset, my house, as collateral, I decided to seek equity investors who would receive ownership in the company for their investment.

I prepared a list of carefully selected venture capital (VC) firms from Silicon Valley to the East Coast and proceeded to contact them with my spectacular story. The response was dismal. I failed to account for the following: knowledge that the economy was struggling with rising unemployment, growing debt, higher taxes, and lower stock prices; VCs were coming off the greater than 20 percent return of the eighties and suffering reversals; less than 1 percent of new businesses were funded by VCs; less than 5 percent of VC investments go to women; my request for a $200,000 investment was too small to attract their interest.

The cost of a small deal is similar to a large one, and thus, its cost becomes a large percentage of the total investment. Also, my location in Cleveland worked against me with the most likely VCs being from Silicon Valley. It seemed risky enough to them without having to travel all the way to Cleveland.

In June of 1990, I presented to the North Coast Growth Capital Conference sponsored by the Weatherhead School of Management and by the local VC community. Even though I aroused little interest, staying in Cleveland made the most sense for me. Here I was near people who knew me. I had a family and a respectable support system. The cost of living in Silicon Valley would have sunk me. In Cleveland, I could find lower costs for rent, furnishings, equipment, and employees.

Little did I know at the time that the refusals from the VCs were a blessing in disguise. My next option was to seek "angel investors," a nice name for the three Fs: family, friends, and fools. Seeking investment from family was not an option. My upbringing had taught me that you never take money from friends. I decided to reach out not to my best friends but to my acquaintances. These were people who knew me, but not in an intimate or dependent way. They knew me well enough to believe that I was honest, relatively conservative, sane, and not likely to risk all for a business that didn't have a high probability for success.

These acquaintances were very unlikely to understand my technology and its potential in the world of electronics. Therefore, they would have to base their investing decision on their trust in me as a worthy person and my ability to explain my business idea. As I began to network and reach out to neighbors, professionals, business owners, accountants, and attorneys, I discovered an attorney who agreed to prepare a Private Placement Memorandum on a contingency basis, meaning, that he would not get paid until I brought in some money.

A Private Placement Memorandum is a document that describes the nature of the investment, the dollar to percent ownership ratio, and defines the risks. This signed document allows me to take money from individuals with minimum risk to myself. Signing this agreement would indicate that the investor understands that it is 100 percent risk and that losing the money invested would not be a hardship. In other words, the investor had to declare that he is a qualified investor and able to take such a risk. This document, coupled with the business plan and a shareholder's agreement, became my tool for raising money. A shareholder's agreement, also called a stockholder's agreement, is an arrangement between the shareholders of a corporation defining the rights and responsibilities of the shareholders and share ownership and valuation. A template for a shareholder's agreement can be found online.

CHAPTER NINE

OPERATIONAL NIGHTMARES

Beware of people bearing gifts, for there is no free lunch.

My home became my initial place of business. Concurrently, while raising money, I was engaged with securing a place to continue development of the technology. While at BP, I had connected with a company developing and making pressure sensitive adhesives (PSAs.) This company was important to me because they built a piece of equipment that could help me manufacture my products. They used it as a laminator. I determined that the nature of this "laminator" could be adapted for calendaring or forming of the Thermagon materials.

In the spring of 1990, the company's owner offered me use of a small corner of his production space to conduct my work for very low rent. It was tight, all of eleven by fourteen feet. The facility was in the snow belt on the far eastside of Cleveland. I lived in Lakewood, forty to fifty miles away. Nonetheless, I was excited to have this space as well as access to the laminating equipment. I could fill in with additional equipment as I saw fit. I was very grateful! I was concerned, however, about how I was going to, personally, maintain myself. I had a house, but it required gas, electricity, water, and, at the very least, a minimum of maintenance. Traveling back and forth to work was expensive, considering the cost of gas and car repairs. My car was old.

After several months of commuting, I came up with the idea to rent out my big old Lakewood house and rent an apartment or condo near my work. I would try to live on the difference in rents. I engineered the plan and ended up with a $700 difference in rents, which became my living expense budget.

Soon I became a regular visitor of the used industrial equipment outlets, where I could pick up a couple machines at a very low price. Such visits were quite an adventure. I started calling them rust warehouses, for they were dark, dank, and without heat. Utilities were at a minimum. I was probably their first female customer. Evaluating a used laminating press would be a challenge for I needed to understand the flatness and surface condition of the platens. I would arrive with white computer paper and carbon paper to put between the platens. Once pressure was applied the imprint on the paper would tell me where the platens made contact and give me some clue as to their flatness. The salesman just stood by and rolled his eyes. When refurbishing or repairing were needed one of my old friends from the BP mechanical shop at the research laboratory would do the work at a reasonable price. My mother loaned me the money to purchase one of the laminators from the PSA business. Slowly but surely, I was beginning to make progress in acquiring the essential production equipment for developing the high thermally conductive products.

Just to be clear, my small space in the back corner of the production area of the PSA plant had no walls, no phones, and no chairs. As I recall, the rent was affordable at $40 per month. What I did have was plenty of "heavy metal," and I don't mean sophisticated production equipment but rather rock music constantly playing in the background from morning to night. During this time, the business owner found a financial partner and was busy putting an addition on his existing building for a PSA coater. As a result, in early 1991, I moved into a ten-by-twenty-five foot space with walls, a desk, and a phone. Now I could sensibly proceed with some sort of a marketing effort. As time passed, my efforts were becoming more and more resource limited. The current economic climate was not conducive to finding investors.

By mid-1991, my lease arrangement had soured. I had been tasked with helping secure the coater from my landlord's former employer for his new addition, not with money but with negotiation as a middleman. That was fine with me, but then he tasked me with babysitting his employees. I was thrown in the back-production area with said employees, and before long we became friends, not to mention very loyal to one another. No way was I tattling on them to the boss.

Then after my landlord had the new space finished and the coater working, I observed that he was slowly and methodically plotting to push his partner out. On top of which, he requested that I start cleaning the bathrooms as part of my rent, often accusing me of not fulfilling the task. It was becoming obvious to me that he had ulterior motives for having me there. I realized that I could very well be the next one to get pushed out or compromised. I suppose that he thought if he backed me into a corner with little to no resources, he would end up with my business. He knew, unquestionably, that I could not afford to pay any increased rent and therefore thought that he could make me more and more dependent on him. More dependence would mean that he could take control. He went so far as to accuse me of stealing. After one year of living in the eastern suburbs, moving back into my house in Lakewood seemed to make sense. I knew I had to make a change in order to protect myself and continue progressing with the business.

So what was my takeaway from this experience with the owner of the PSA business and other incidents with potential investors? For anyone, particularly a woman, to appear needy makes them exceedingly vulnerable.

To accomplish my goals with minimal resources limited my options for a successful path forward. Not only was I lacking financial resources to physically start the business, but I was also lacking advisory resources to help me make good decisions. I found that I had to continually be on my guard. Many of the options presented were not in my best interest. When people offered me help, being aware of what they expected in return became very important. "Beware of people bearing gifts," became my motto.

Most businessmen, and they were all men, perceived a woman as someone who probably didn't understand what she had, how to promote it, or how to attract investors. I perceived that many of the men who offered to assist me were thinking of a way to take control of my business and, ultimately, claim ownership. My plan to seek investors from acquaintances that I had some history and knowledge of turned out to be a sound decision. The truth being that most all businesspeople are looking for a deal to advance their own business, often with little concern for the impact on their adversary. My image as a petite blond with minimal business experience was not one that men, in my day, would perceive as a successful businessperson. Making an advantageous deal with me may have seemed like easy pickings. Hiding my desperate need for support was extremely difficult in those early years. My recommendation for those female entrepreneurs trying to start a business with limited resources is to surround yourself with trusted advisors who are smart businesspeople. Also, I would recommend to never appear flirtatious in business meetings. I consider myself quite fortunate to have avoided decisions that could have had very bad outcomes. I created a much stronger advisory network in the coming years. I also learned that successful business deals need to be a win-win, not a situation where one party takes advantage of another.

By early 1992, I had laid the groundwork, I hoped, for propelling Thermagon forward to a successful product launch and profitability. I was still in survival mode with no income. I had moved back into my old house in Lakewood, so the $700 income per month was gone. Threats from BP were still a possibility, but with each passing year, they seemed less likely. My networking endeavors with second-tier friends, combined with the business plan and associated legal documents, had surfaced several potential investors. My place of business in the PSA company had served its purpose in the progress of Thermagon even though a physical move was imperative. Concerns of vulnerability continued.

My oldest son's fiancée, Susan, who was attending college during the early stage of Thermagon, worked for me as a volunteer. She learned how to test our products, as well as competitive products for thermal resistance. She was instrumental in helping create one of our products that later became quite successful. More importantly, she shared the little successes of Thermagon with my son, Jim, who, ultimately, had the courage to join me and become an integral part of the company.

Several potential new products had been formulated and tested. I had acquired a manufacturer's representative; a person assigned a specific geographic area in which he was granted exclusive rights to sell certain products on a commission basis in Silicon Valley. Manufacturer's representatives, otherwise known as reps, are found through networking within the thermal management community. Could I now find the resources to propel the company forward?

Launching the Company

The Start-Up Phase of Thermagon

CHAPTER TEN

MOVING THE NEEDLE
OFF ZERO

A strong sense of urgency is imperative.

The start-up phase of Thermagon happened between 1992 and 1994. The economy was taking off with 3 to 4 percent per year growth. An average of 1.7 million jobs were being created annually, compared to 850,000 per year during the century. Unemployment dropped from 8 percent to 4 percent, and stocks quadrupled in value. This tremendous growth in the economy can be contributed to many factors, not the least of which was the technological revolution. The World Wide Web was leading to the advent of the internet. The Clean Air Act and concerns about pollution, particularly in California, led to the revival of the electric car. In 1993, Intel launched its exclusive Pentium brand of microprocessors. The Pentium's contribution to technological development enabled the types of computer applications that we take for granted today. It was becoming clear to me that the world of electronics would soon need the heat transfer capability of the Thermagon products.

Through word of mouth, I learned that the owner of an old building on West Twenty-Fifth Street was possibly willing to rent out a small space. The rent was affordable at $500 per month. Nothing was really *affordable* for me at that point. Luckily, I exited the eastside location unscathed for the owner did not show up the day I moved. It turned out my new landlord was a gem. He allowed me to use his office equipment in the beginning, much like a business incubator. The 1,200-square-foot space was L-shaped in the front corner of the second floor. I took little notice of the operation outside my office, where disadvantaged people made refrigerator magnets and key chains. I thought it was paradise.

One of the more memorable occasions was right after I occupied the space. One of my potential investors stopped by to pay a visit with his son. I suddenly realized I had no chairs for them to sit down in. I quickly scampered about the building and borrowed a couple of chairs. The gentleman, ultimately, invested and was quick to remind me, from time to time, about the dilemma of no chairs. Soon I learned of the availability of some office furniture (i.e., tables, chairs, desks, storage) for little money. My son Jim had a pickup truck and moved the furniture into the building. It was a start. I was determined to turn my space into a high-tech operation. I now had enough space for some production, development, and testing, as well as some offices.

Wonderful!

Thankfully, I did not have many customer-type visits in those early years for the neighborhood and setting was a bit daunting. My need for investors could not have been greater. I had a few meager sales in 1991 totaling about $5,000. I was smart enough to understand that that was not significant in the scheme of things. My very first sale was to IBM for a sample of a molded epoxy material that I doubted would become mainstream. The sale was for $100.

A different division of IBM purchased some epoxy adhesive films for circuit board laminate. This technology was very much in development. Also, I made a new material for Aavid Engineering who were looking for cheap materials with average thermal performance. For them, I developed a product called T-dux. None of these sales represented what Thermagon was capable of doing. I refrained from any excitement. I had survived well into the third year without an income. If it had not been for the rent-differential money, an occasional few hundred dollars for some consulting work, some pension money from BP (as I recall about $18,000), and the loan from my mother to purchase the forming rolls, I certainly would not have made it this far. My strategy to reach out to acquaintances rather than close friends proved to be effective.

By March of 1992, I was equipped with all the necessary documents to make a very professional presentation to potential investors. Included in the package were the following:

1. Private placement memorandum
2. Summary of the offering
3. Business plan
4. Articles of incorporation of Thermagon
5. Code of regulations
6. Shareholders' agreement
7. Subscription agreement

Thermagon was chartered November 3, 1989, enabling me as its principal owner to address the electronic industry's need for thermally conductive, electrically insulating polymeric materials (TCPM) for improving heat transfer, thus reducing product failure rates. Up to one hundred shares of common stock of Thermagon at $2,000 per share was offered. Immediately, prior to the offering, two hundred shares of Thermagon stock was outstanding in the name of Carol Latham, the founder and CEO. If all offered shares were sold, three hundred shares would be outstanding. The minimum size of the offering is thirty-five shares. The minimum investment was five shares or $10,000. It was a closing condition of this offering that the company shall receive subscriptions (but not payment) for thirty-five shares before accepting any payment. All investors would need to acknowledge by signature that they understood all risks, including the illiquidity and lack of transferability of the shares.

By the end of April 1992, I had five investors: three people subscribing to five shares each and two people subscribing to ten shares each. I was now able to accept my first investment money for the sale of thirty-five shares for $70,000. Ultimately, I think that these first five investors considered themselves geniuses, and believe me, I would never have disagreed. In my mind, they were saints!

The group was comprised of an entrepreneur who made his money in the coal business; a businessman who was president of the Medical Center Company, managing the physical plant for Case Western University and University Hospital; a retired bank executive who was a friend of my ex-husband, a tennis friend, and accountant who did the Thermagon financial statements for many years; and a housewife who was independently affluent and wanted to make her own investment independent of her husband.

Having a nucleus of investors certainly made it easier to attract others. By the end of 1992, I had three additional investors, purchasing twenty additional shares for $40,000, and by May 1993, three others had invested, purchasing another fifteen shares for $30,000. Basically, the additional shareholders were friends and acquaintances of the original five investors and one of my original employees. At our first shareholders' meeting in May of 1993, I announced that the stock offering would be closing in fairness to all who had invested. The current investors immediately offered to purchase the remaining shares. That was a great vote of confidence for me. Yes, success was a long time coming!

Now let the work begin! It is mid-1992. My investors recommended people they knew who were unemployed for potential employees of Thermagon. Not only was our situation very risky for the investors, but it was also risky for job security. Enticing people to commit to work for Thermagon was a sales challenge all its own. First off, two people who were unemployed agreed to come work for Thermagon. I won them over by proposing that each of us, including me, would earn $1,000 per month in salary. Even in 1992, that was extremely low. I emphasized that we were in this venture together and that we would win together. These two gentlemen took a risk, along with the investors, I proceeded to train them on how to make our products. Six months or so later, my daughter-in-law, Susan, joined the company as my willing-to-do-anything assistant. Fantastic!

The Thermagon products are a mixture of ceramic fillers and polymers. The resulting composite needs to have high thermal conductivity, be electrically insulating, formable into sheets, soft, and have integrity for easy handling. As I have pointed out previously, the

Thermagon materials have a high thermal conductivity compared to all others in the marketplace. However, that is only part of the equation. The bottom line is to have the thermal resistance from the device to the heat spreader (a metal device that ranges from a plate to a finned part often with a fan attached) as low as possible. Air is a thermal insulator. The goal is to replace the air at the interface between the device and heat spreader with minimal pressure and material thickness. Imagine that the magnified surfaces you are mating resemble the palms of your hands. By putting your hands together, you will realize that they are only touching in a few areas, and much air is entrapped between. Thermagon's materials are designed to fill that gap as completely as possible and obtain the lowest possible thermal resistance.

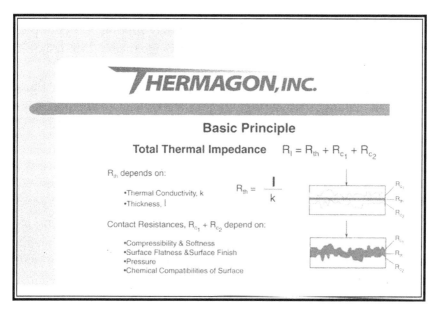

The thermal resistance of the composite material itself is the thermal conductivity divided by the thickness for a given area. Therefore, high thermal conductivity and minimal thickness will give you the lowest thermal resistance of the material itself. However, the total thermal resistance across an interface is the sum of the resistance of the material plus the contact resistance at each interface.

These contact resistances are dependent on the pressure applied to the assembly, the softness or compressibility of the material, the surface finish and flatness of the mating parts. Thermagon's materials not only had high thermal conductivity but were softer than any in the marketplace, thus allowing for minimal thermal resistance at low pressures. Most of Thermagon's materials were supplied in sheet form or as pads. However, we did supply some paste encapsulants, adhesives, and greases.

The thermal conductivity of our materials was mostly dependent on the properties of the ceramic powders and the process for manufacturing them. Since the products could not be reverse engineered, we were able to keep our technology as trade secrets. The bulk of our products were made into sheets of various thermal conductivities, thicknesses, and compressibility. The sheets were then die-cut into the exact footprint of the device they were cooling. For example, our premium product was made in ten mil increments from ten mils to two hundred mils. (Products on page 74.)

Thermagon also supplied thermally conductive adhesive films for use in making thermally conductive printed circuit boards. These products were our most difficult challenge. Basically, these materials provided a means for making metal-based circuit boards for maximum heat transfer. The films needed to be almost as thin as a piece of paper, consistent in thickness across the sheet, strong adhesives, withstand the circuit board industry chemicals, and have very good electrically insulating properties. And oh yes, be thermally conductive! Most would think this is impossible.

As Thermagon continued to develop new products to stay ahead of the curve for always providing the best solution for the most difficult heat issues, we constantly needed to think outside the box. One example is the T-putty material we designed for Teradyne, a manufacturer of semiconductor test equipment. The material was exceedingly soft with high thermal conductivity and was manufactured totally in reverse of all logic, adding the boron nitride filler to the silicone gel after it was cured. The resulting product was a big hit!

Our product line was developed by listening to our potential and existing customers and providing materials that solved their thermal problems. Without a sales and marketing/travel budget, Thermagon needed to find creative ways to reach potential customers. The number one thing that we did was place "new product releases" in technical journals. That meant sending blurbs about our products to all the many technical journals relating to electronic systems, not just once but repeatedly until the blurb was published. In the beginning, the blurb was all words and no pictures. Making copy with photography was too expensive. Generally in those days, electronic design engineers picked up their journal and went directly to the back to learn about what was new from the "new product releases." Once the new blurb about one of our products was printed, the interested design engineers would circle the number corresponding to our product on a "bingo card." The numbers of all the "new product releases" were printed on this "bingo card" with the engineer's name, company, address, and phone number. Once the engineer circled the product numbers of those he was interested in, he would mail the card back to the journal. The journal, in turn, would compile a list of names, companies, addresses, and phone numbers, then mail the list to the companies supplying the "new product releases."

The greatest thing about this process was that it was free, except for a little postage. I would phone each engineer on the list and learn about their thermal issue. Common questions I asked were "what material are you using now?" "Why are you looking for something different?" Then I would ask them to try one of our products in their system and determine for themselves the thermal advantage we had to offer. By learning about their application, I would suggest a product or products and ship them to the engineer overnight—free of charge. Our sense of urgency and immediate response won over many engineers, and the results of their testing would soon follow. Our data sheets that accompanied our products were printed on letterhead paper on our computer printer—not a very professional look. It was what we could afford, and in reality, the engineers could not have cared less.

Often these discussions would lead to the development of new products. One example was Schlumberger who I initially sent our highest performing premium product. They tested it and responded that it was not soft enough. Almost every day, for many weeks, I would send a new product overnight until finally one material was working satisfactorily in Schlumberger's system. The resulting product was T-putty. T-putty turned out to have the highest profit margin of all our products. How to ship this very soft T-putty became the next challenge.

T-putty was made to a prescribed thickness, and if anything touched it, the material would smush and not maintain its original thickness. We developed a way to use strips of cardboard stacked higher than the sheets of T-putty, as well as placed in between the T-putty sheets, so that when we placed another layer of sheets above, they would not touch. The method worked and our sheets arrived safely intact.

The other trick I used in talking to the engineers was to introduce myself as the technical director, never as the CEO. I always wanted to give the impression that Thermagon was larger than it really was. Fortune 500 companies are not likely to give business to such a small company. The companies in Silicon Valley were most likely to be interested in new products and immediate results rather than worrying about the company's size. On the other hand, companies on the East Coast were likely to want to know the companies' pedigree before they would consent to do business with you. Thank goodness for the entrepreneurial spirit of Silicon Valley.

Initially, I was the one taking phone calls and communicating with customers and potential customers. It was several years before I could afford to travel and meet them in person. As the company began to grow, a decision needed to be made concerning how we would develop a sales force. Early on, I had the good fortune to find a manufacturers' representative (rep) in Silicon Valley. He was most helpful in connecting us with potential customers. Soon he was generating business. As is typical with reps, they are paid a percentage of the purchase order price once the sale is made. Since we had cash flow concerns, this worked very well for us—so well, in fact, that we built a rep network across the country to sell our products. The rep organizations we worked with were all independent companies who represented a certain geographic area. We found them by networking with other material and component suppliers into the electronics industry. Hiring full-time salespeople would be very costly and could well have been the demise of the company.

Having established the company name very early in the evolution of Thermagon, one of my friends had a son who was a student at Cleveland Institute of Art. He developed my original logo, which dramatized the "T" in Thermagon, as it was scripted across the paper. From that, I proceeded to name all the Thermagon products with a lead letter "T." For example, T-gon, the first one represented several of our early products that were differentiated with a numbering system. For example, our insulating product for power supplies was called T-gon—210. The last two digits represented the thickness of the material in mils (thousandths of an inch). A product developed for Aavid Engineering was called T-dux. Soon we had T-pli. As we developed new products, all their names were preceded by the letter "T."

In addition to the many accomplishments of Thermagon in 1992, life's events and maladies were going on in the background. In June, Jim got married. Weddings with no resources are also tricky. The wedding was in my backyard with the kids handling the food and I the decor and decoration. Lady Luck gave us a beautiful day, so the tent was barely needed.

In November, I ruptured my Achilles tendon playing tennis. That meant two months of a cast and crutches. I had just received some major orders from Schlumberger and panicked as I got the bad news. My three employees rallied around and supported me through the ordeal without a missed delivery. This was winter with much ice and snow. I could only get into my office by using a wheelchair in the freight elevator. One of my employees would meet me at the car with the wheelchair and transport me to my office, where I would discard the wheelchair and motor with crutches. It wasn't long until I taught myself to drive left-footed so that no one needed to drive me back and forth to work. The trickiest day was when the elevator broke. Navigating long staircases on crutches takes some dexterity.

After the two months were up and the cast was removed, I had the task of learning to walk again. I learned that life can go on successfully even under such difficulties. Thanks to a collaborative effort, sales in 1992 were close to $75,000. The good news was that our new product, T-pli, accounted for more than half of the sales. I was hopeful that we had a winning product with T-pli.

Below is a summary list of the accomplishments of 1992.

1. Moved into our new space on West Twenty-Fifth Street
2. Found investors to provide the resources to launch the company
3. Formed a board of directors
4. Added three full-time employees, plus myself, made four
5. Could now focus on promoting and selling our products
6. Acquired a manufacturers' representative in Silicon Valley
7. Had sufficient equipment to manufacture small orders
8. Had simple thermal testing equipment in place to support R&D and quality control
9. Our product offerings grew to five
10. Leading our customer list were companies such as Schlumberger, Silicon Graphics, Advanced Logic Research, Aavid Engineering, Sun Microsystems, and Hughes Aircraft.
11. Sales totaled $75,000 with an operating loss of $24,000

Funny and Interesting Antidote

One of our early design wins for T-pli was for cooling a high-end computer at Silicon Graphics, or so I thought. To be "designed in" means that the product, T-pli, is specified on the drawing used for assembling the Silicon Graphics device.

One day, I answered the telephone to a gruff voice asking, "Is this Thermagon? How the hell was I supposed to find you?" We were a young company, still with very low visibility and, therefore, difficult to find. Soon to learn, I was speaking with Rocky from Rocky's Gasket Shop.

Silicon Graphics, as it turned out, used Rocky's Gasket Shop to cut their parts to the desired shape and apply them to their heat spreader. A gasket shop? Who would have ever guessed?

Thinking I was launching this high-tech company, I didn't expect to be bowing to the wishes of a guy named Rocky. I was soon to get down off my pedestal and realize that this is how business was done. Whether Rocky's wife was related to an executive of Silicon Graphics, I will never know. I ultimately met Rocky, and we had a great business relationship.

Moral to the story—always keep an open mind and respect the little guy.

CHAPTER ELEVEN

MAINTAINING THE MOMENTUM

Don't be afraid to cross boundaries, for creativity and innovation come from combining unlike things.

We started 1993 with four employees and ended 1994 with seven, despite the fact that we lost two in 1993. We lost one to a wife who was transferred out of town, and the other was my daughter-in-law, Susan. She became pregnant with my first grandchild. She continued to work until days before she gave birth. She told me many times that after she gave birth to my first grandchild, she would not come back. I was not a believer, but she held true to her word. She helped us out many times in the years to follow but never returned to her former position. Our new employees included the following:

> ➤ A printed circuit board expert, who had started a printed circuit board shop at an early age and ran into difficulties. His job was to manage the adhesive film product that was slated to make thermally conductive metal-based circuit boards.
> ➤ A technician to work in production who had lost his ham franchise business.

> ➢ Jim who now had a wife and baby. This was a monumental decision for me to agree to bring him on board. He had been looking to make a change from his existing position and was finding it was harder than he thought. For me, I had been in survival mode for the past five years and taking on, not only my son, but his family was very daunting. I insisted that the medical insurance was signed, sealed, and delivered before I would give the nod of okay.

> ➢ A technician from Jim's former company, who helped in production and worked with me on R&D.

> ➢ My youngest son, Craig, a recent graduate of Kent State University in history, was eagerly searching for his place in this world and a respectable job. I made it quite clear to him that any task in the company was fair game. He assumed many administrative tasks, including becoming our bookkeeper and liaison to our accountants. Having a family member managing the money was very comforting for me.

To have my sons involved in the business was never contemplated and was a great bonus. With the increase in sales and a brighter outlook for the future, I felt comfortable in increasing the pay scale of all the employees from the original $1,000 stipend per month to nearer market value.

In these two years, we were able to enhance the sales and marketing effort as follows:

1. Upgraded our sales and product literature with a better computer-generated version
2. Began to travel nationally to meet with customers and potential customers
3. Placed two paid advertisements in separate trade journals
4. Participated in our first trade show
5. Acquired new sales representatives for New England and Pacific Northwest

6. Considered creating a thermally conductive circuit board laminate division of Thermagon

We continued to develop new products to satisfy the needs of our customers. This development work was still solely in my hands at this point. I was in contact with the customers and working with the help of one technician to create these new products. The thrust of the interface materials was to maintain high thermal conductivity and make them softer—not an easy task. Also, we were developing laminate structures using our adhesive film. I was responsible for the film development, and our new circuit board expert was responsible for the structures.

In the development of the Thermagon products, trials were made using many fillers to determine which would provide the highest thermal conductivity. My competitors used aluminum oxide (alumina) almost exclusively. Improving thermal conductivity using alumina as a filler was certainly not my chosen path. My trials using boron nitride (BN) achieved the unexpected results I was hoping for. As a part of this work, I tried every BN powder available in the world. I soon learned that only the US suppliers had powders that could produce high thermal conductivity. The US suppliers are Carborundum in Niagara Falls, New York, and Union Carbide in Cleveland, Ohio. Their processes for making BN are quite different. One certain powder from Carborundum stood out above all the rest for providing the most thermally conductive materials.

As my investors became more knowledgeable about the Thermagon business, one concern they often expressed was my sole sourcing of this special powder. My premium product, T-pli, used this powder. In 1993, news became public that Dan T. Moore, a local entrepreneur, had purchased the boron nitride business from Union Carbide. I promptly wrote him a letter and explained that I was building a business on BN and suggested that we meet. Dan responded positively and came to Thermagon for a visit. I was hoping he would not react negatively to my modest facility.

Soon I became involved with the technical staff of Advanced Ceramics (as the business was now called) with the hopes of their developing a powder that would perform better in my process. Many years and many trials later, we managed to use their powders in some products but never for our highest thermal conductivity.

In addition to our new employees, our new product development, our enhanced marketing efforts, and our raw material evaluations, Thermagon's probability of success was increased by its raw material intensive business model and its pricing strategy. Most manufacturing companies are capital intensive, meaning, the amount of capital expenditures required is high in relation to the labor and raw material costs. For example, think about oil refining, circuit board manufacturing, and even a printing business. All require large outlays of capital to purchase the machinery to fulfill their objective. Also, complicated machinery requires maintenance and may often need replacing for the business to remain state of the art.

Thermagon, on the other hand, was not capital intensive. The manufacturing equipment purchased was mostly used with price tags less than $50,000. The roll laminators were purchased new but cost about $10,000 each. This proved quite affordable, and we could avoid going into debt. The process could be likened to a kitchen with mixing, forming into sheets and curing with heat and pressure. We had purchased two roll laminators, a laminating press and larger mixer, and some test equipment by the end of 1994. Even though the manufacturing process was a batch process rather than continuous, the labor cost to produce the products was about 15 percent of revenue and about one third of the total of cost of goods sold and trending downward. The Thermagon products could be considered raw material intensive. Particularly in our high thermal conductivity products, the BN filler powders are quite expensive. I used to tell the production workers that each time they took a scoop full of powder, it cost $100. I was probably not too far off. The workers got the message not to be wasteful. The material cost as a percentage of revenue was dependent on the product mix but was trending up as the labor costs were trending down. Our raw material cost was our most expensive variable; hence, the products were considered raw material intensive.

Knowing how to price the products was key to our success. I controlled the pricing for the entire duration of the company. First, I needed to understand exactly the cost of goods sold for each product sheet, usually sixteen by sixteen inches, in every available thickness. Once the sheets were die-cut into the custom shapes, our parts averaged about one to two square inches in area. Therefore, I calculated the cost on dollars per square inch. After making our basic sheets, the process to further customize our products was called converting. The converting process could be done either in-house at Thermagon or by a converter somewhere else in the world. In addition to custom die-cutting, often sheets were required to have pressure sensitive adhesive (PSA) on one side for aid in assembly. Each of these steps were incurred costs. The basic markup before any other factors were taken into consideration was three times. Basic sheet prices did have volume price breaks.

Second, I knew the prices of all our competitive materials. During the sales cycle, I would learn about the customer, his application, his needs for certain properties and usually the material that we were replacing. During the sales cycle and the sampling process, I would always ask the customer what he was currently using to solve his thermal need and why he was considering a new material. With this information I could estimate, based on the price of the competitive product and his thermal need, the highest price his application could bear.

Third, I knew the relative performance of our competitor's products because I had tested them on our test equipment to get comparable data rather than just using their data sheets. The trick was to determine what our "value-add" was worth to the customer in his application. For example, would lower thermal performance lead to equipment failures?

Often our products were the only thermal solution the customer had. Even so, there was a limit as to how high a price the customer could bear. If you are cooling a $20 processor in a $1,000 computer, what is it worth for the processor to not overheat? Common sense would put your price in a reasonable range.

Fourthly, the function of the thermal products to dissipate heat was similar in each application. This function, combined with other needs, such as thickness, softness, elasticity, and tack, would determine the material selection for each customer. The cost of goods sold for the different sheets varied significantly. I learned not to base the sales price solely on the cost of goods sold but rather would base the price also on the customers need and product function.

For example, one customer began the sales cycle testing our pricier product with little concern for its price. After testing the customer said he needed something softer, and so I sent him new samples. Softer yet, he said, and so forth. By the time I arrived at the perfect material solution for him, the cost of goods sold for the chosen material was significantly lower than the first trial material. What should his price be?

Answer: close to the premium product price.

Consequently, as the business grew, our gross profit became greater than 50 percent and sometimes trended upward of 60 percent. My friend and confidant at Aavid Engineering (heat sink supplier) once told me that my products cost "too goddamn much!" I simply ignored him. Years later, he confided, "You are a pricing genius."

Thermagon was about to complete its third full year of operation. Knowing that start-up companies seldom survive their first three years, we were feeling quite fortunate to be alive and gaining ground.

In 1993, we had revenue of $180,000 and managed to break even. In 1994, we had revenue of $365,000 with a net profit of $32,000, 8.7 percent of sales.

Wow, this was exciting! To begin 1995 in the black was truly incredible.

Interface Pads

Gap Fillers

Putties & Greases

Adhesives

Encapsulants

Thermally-Conductive PCBs

_T_HERMAGON, INC.

The Thermal Performance Leader

Transformation of Thermagon

CHAPTER TWELVE

UNEXPECTED OFFER

Making assumptions may be misleading:
It is okay and prudent to state the obvious.

The business had stabilized, orders were coming in, and we were profitable. All companies strive to grow their business. Sales of $365,000 in 1994 were double that of the previous year yet hardly gave Thermagon bragging rights nor a sense of security that we had made it. We were continuing on the path of maintaining our existing customers and reaching out to prospective customers with overnight-free samples of our products, carefully selected to fit best into each specific application. The sales cycle for acquiring a new customer could take six to twelve months. In the first quarter, our sales were flat at best, comparable with sales of first quarter 1994 and down from fourth quarter 1994.

Of note was our account with Schlumberger who made semiconductor test equipment. This equipment consisted of racks full of large printed circuit boards mated to cold plates that were water-cooled. Our very soft T-putty product was used exclusively to mate the heat-generating devices on the circuit boards to the cold plate. Very soft thermally conductive material was needed to fill the varied heights between the cold plate and the devices. Our T-putty product was designed specifically for them. As the semiconductor's growth rate increased, so should our business with Schlumberger grow.

A second account of note was with Cray Computer. They had recently purchased Digital Equipment and were using their technology to make modular high-end computers at affordable prices. Previously, Cray Computer was known for their very high performing and expensive supercomputers. They came to us, asking that we make our premium product in many thicknesses. For example, we made T-pli in .005-inch increments as follows: .010 inches, .015 inches, .020 inches, .025 inches, .030 inches, .035 inches with each thickness a different color. They called their process thermal shimming, whereby they would select the best thickness during the assembly process of each computer to assure maximum heat transfer. This product provided us with a significant piece of business.

Meeting with Arthur Andersen

My shareholders were all successful businesspeople in their own right even though their understanding of Thermagon's technology was a bit sketchy. I welcomed their input into the administrative side of the business, where I was somewhat weak. One of them called, asking if I would be willing to meet with someone he knew from Arthur Anderson (AA), a leading accounting firm. Having agreed, his friend, VP of marketing at AA, and his colleague, Paul, came to Thermagon for a meeting. I explained our business and its current status. Paul appeared to take an interest in our business and openly offered his assistance and phone number to call him anytime with business and accounting issues. Paul became invaluable to me as my confidant and mentor. He stepped in to help with buyout opportunities, the strategy with Saint-Gobain, company succession planning, tax planning, city enterprise programs, and more.

Not only did he help in a significant way, he never billed me for the first couple of years. I believe this story must be told. Quite frankly, if anyone would have told me that AA would donate their services to a start-up company, I would never have believed them. To the best of my understanding, AA was embracing a strategy to help young companies with the hope of developing a major paying client in the future. This was a tremendous windfall.

Encounter with Chomerics

Soon I received a call from Chomerics, one of our major competitors, who stated that they were interested in making an offer to purchase Thermagon. Of course, Thermagon was not for sale, but I needed to hear them out. This became a perfect chance to connect back with AA and Paul. Parker Hannifin had recently purchased Chomerics from W. R. Grace for $40 million. In 1993, Chomerics's sales revenue was $55 million, of which I speculate $15 to 20 million were for thermal interface materials. Chomerics was a major supplier of electromagnetic interference (EMI) shielding materials, as well as their thermal interface materials. I was aware that they knew about the superior performance of our new thermal interface materials. They also knew that I was a single woman who founded and managed the company on my own.

I firmly believed that they thought I was naive enough to sell the company at a quite low price of $5 million. I agreed to a meeting with them in April of 1995. What they did not know was that I had connected with Paul of AA and that he would be accompanying me to the meeting. I had my "ducks all in a row," as did Paul.

Dressed in my red suit and somewhat versed in the history of the small town of Woburn, Massachusetts, where Chomerics resided, I was able to capture the attention of the company executives present at the meeting. Even though Paul and I had not known each other for very long and had never presented together before, we played off one another very well. I told the Thermagon story as much as I was willing to share, and Paul provided the financial projections that demonstrated that $5 million was far too low even for our least aggressive projections. We left them speechless by the end of the meeting. How could this small company of about half a million dollars in sales be worth so much? The low, medium, and high sales projections all justified a considerably higher price for the Thermagon business. The high profitability of the business certainly was a contributing factor.

As I left the meeting to return to Cleveland, I knew the Chomerics executives were stunned, not only by the professional manner in which we presented ourselves but also by the boldness of our optimistic projections. I felt proud and full of renewed confidence. I truly believe Chomerics thought they could convince me to sell at a $5 million price tag. The question remained, "Would they make a counter offer?"

After the meeting, they retreated and tried every available option to crack our trade secrets. For example, at trade shows, they would show up in the booth next to ours with the hopes that they could eavesdrop and learn some secrets. They attempted to use my Carborundum patent to solve the riddle but learned that was impossible. They never made another offer. I believe that competition makes all companies more innovative and stronger. Thermagon and Chomerics continued their business lives as true competitors.

CHAPTER THIRTEEN

UNEXPECTED SURGE

Often one must act without all pertinent facts.

Over the short life of Thermagon, I tried to connect with Intel, but finding the correct connection in such a large company was difficult. I was not aware that anyone from Intel had asked Thermagon for samples. Since I was still handling the incoming customer calls, I was quite certain that they had never reached out to us. One day, the phone rang, and it was Rakesh from Intel. I was very surprised! Rakesh, nonchalantly, with no reference to positive test results, asked me if I could supply them with our premium product T-pli, along with the data sheets. They explained they were going to Asia in ten days and wanted to take them along.

"Of course, I can supply the samples," I replied.

"Oh, and by the way, do you have a sales agent in Taiwan? We need to be able to tell our customers how to purchase your products."

"No," I replied, unequivocally. That task had yet to make my to-do list. Even so, I immediately responded that I would find such a sales agent ASAP. Apparently, unbeknownst to me, Intel ran their own tests on my T-pli product and were impressed with the results. Intel was not known for giving out compliments. Expressing an interest was all that was needed.

In retrospect, maybe my new manufacturer representative in Silicon Valley, where Intel's headquarters resides, had dropped some samples off to them. I was soon to learn that Intel's thermal laboratory was in Arizona.

In the moment, the unbelievable impact on Thermagon generated by this phone call was incomprehensible. The impact was overshadowed by the immediate tasks and concerns about addressing Intel's needs. The samples were easy for us to assemble and ship, but the data sheets were still very raw and unprofessionally generated from my computer printer. If Intel realized how small we were, they might retreat. The actual engineers did not seem to be troubled by the look of our data sheets but rather were intent on the data provided.

All good news!

The need for a sales agent in Taiwan led to an immediate global search for a likely prospect. Common perceptions of Taiwanese businessmen created a paranoia about their trustworthiness. Through my colleagues in the thermal world of electronics, I received a recommendation for a sales agent in Taiwan. I knew very little about him, except that he had worked with a colleague of mine in the heat-pipe business. He agreed to fill the role. However, he would not sign a manufacturer's representative agreement, saying that he only worked on trust and a handshake. I had little recourse but to comply. Well, I was shaking in my shoes, more nervous than ever. Nevertheless, I gave his name to Intel as our newly acquired sales agent named DJ. It was quite common for Asian men to go by initials since their given names were often difficult to pronounce and remember. I was soon to learn that DJ received his degree in thermal engineering in the United States and that his English was comprehensible. DJ, an entrepreneur and founder of his company, Enertron, is smart and definitely knows his way around the electronic manufacturers in Taiwan, particularly in notebook computers.

A good start!

Technology in the nineties was dominated by computer science with the advent of the World Wide Web. Computers were not yet smart enough or fast enough to realize the web's potential. That is until Intel entered the fray with its exclusive brand of Pentium microprocessors in 1993. They enabled the types of computer applications that we take for granted today. The computer industry went from computers filling entire air-conditioned rooms to personal computers that fit underneath your desk to, now, the introduction of portable laptop computers.

As the functionality and speed of the processing ramped up and the physical size of computers dramatically decreased, heat now became the limiting factor to progress. Enter Thermagon! Now with the recognition from Intel, there was nothing stopping us. I was soon to learn that Intel would not be our customer, but rather it would be the manufacturers of the computers themselves, such as Dell, Compaq, IBM, and many others or their contract manufacturers. Intel's role was to specify Thermagon's T-pli material in their design guide for using their Pentium microprocessors.

Over the next two quarters of 1995, computer manufacturers were working through the engineering and sales process of specifying our materials into their products with the help of DJ. He seemed to understand that we were a young start-up company and that cash flow would be a big problem as we began to grow. As a result, he instructed me to hold many of the initial orders until I received payment.

Unbelievable!

Usually, you would be fortunate to receive payment in thirty days, if not sixty or ninety days. In other words, he was looking out for my well-being, and we had yet to meet. Our business relationship continued to grow positively. Ultimately, he became a strong confidant and ambassador for our products in Asia. It was a win-win situation. We are friends to this day.

By the fourth quarter of 1995, our sales began to take off with nearly half of our yearly sales occurring in the fourth quarter. This growth was attributed mainly to our material used with Intel's Pentium chip in notebook computers. Since Thermagon's inception, credibility had always been a major issue and cause for concern. With Intel's endorsement, Thermagon gained immediate recognition and indisputable respect. Even though it was not immediately obvious the day of the call, Thermagon would now receive inquiries from many aspects of the electronics industry, not directly related to personal computers. In other words, Intel put our name on the map as a leader in thermal interface materials.

Experiencing an event that triggers sudden and rapid growth is truly exciting. Managing such sudden and rapid growth can be very daunting. Many companies fail as the result of such an experience. Everything from your production capabilities, your systems development, your supply chain, your advisory support, and your sales channels must be strategically developed and managed effectively. Several key factors helped Thermagon along its growth path.

Our sudden and explosive growth could not have had successful outcomes without the input and efforts of both of my sons. Jim, a mechanical engineer, was ideally suited to take over the manufacture of our products. He excelled in design and organization. This brings one humorous story to mind. When Jim arrived, I was doing my best to hold things together. In order to provide a diemaker with a drawing to produce a needed die, I would get out my architect's rule and a pencil and draw the pattern.

"Oh my," Jim exclaimed. "That will never do."

At that point in his life, he had some experience with AutoCAD. We both laughed. That was just one of the many processes Jim impacted. Craig, on the other hand, began his work with Thermagon mostly on the administrative side of the business.

One day, Jim decided that we needed a computer program to help manage the business. In walked Craig to research and develop a program. In these early days of computers, the term information technology (IT) was nonexistent. Before too long, Craig had devised a system and database that helped us manage the multiple functions of Thermagon. He ultimately became our IT expert, along with many other responsibilities.

Thermagon ended 1995 with seven full-time and two part-time employees and a sales revenue of $645,000, with nearly half of the sales coming in the last quarter. Our gross profit was $250,000, about 40 percent of sales. Our net profit was $160,000, about 25 percent of sales. Thermagon ended the year with optimism for the future and anticipated growth!

THE GROWTH
YEARS

1996–2000

CHAPTER FOURTEEN

MANAGING CHANGE

*Change is inevitable! How one manages
change will determine the outcomes.*

Thermagon began the process of a tremendous transformation. Change was the order of the day. How I and my Thermagon colleagues reacted to and managed change would control our destiny. Technology transfer from me to my employees became critical. To succeed the company needed to be much bigger than myself. Letting go is difficult for entrepreneurs and often leads to failure if not successfully executed.

The hardest for me was to transfer my interface with the customers over to others. All employees, including myself, needed to successfully take on new roles and skills as well as seeking expertise from outside. A "can-do" attitude dominated the day-to-day operation. Employees learned quickly to never tell me something can't be done.

This transformation of Thermagon to a recognized real company can be summarized as follows:

1. Sales grew from less than $1 million to nearly $19 million with an expanded customer base from mostly computer related to other industries, such as telecommunications and with a demographic shift from mostly in United States to 40 percent international. Marketing and applications engineering efforts grew through the work of a staff of four.

2. Travel became a priority particularly as international business grew.

3. With the need for higher volume and more efficient manufacturing, physical space expanded from 6,800 square feet in our existing location to 20,000 square feet and then grew further through the purchase of our own building with 50,000 square feet.

4. Employees grew from seven to 120 with the company creating a very unique culture.

5. Research and development effort expanded to a staff of four to five, led by a PhD from Advanced Ceramics.

6. Organization changed from a mom-and-pop shop to a real corporate structure.

7. Expanded our list of companies interested in acquiring Thermagon from just Chomerics to more than ten.

8. Gained much notoriety and recognition.

CHAPTER FIFTEEN

SALES AND MARKETING

Getting closer than ever to your customers, so
close, in fact, that you tell them what they need
before they realize it themselves.

—Steve Jobs, founder of Apple

I n 1996, sales grew fourfold to $2.4 million as a result of the Intel
endorsement of our T-pli material. Our customers for T-pli were
notebook computer manufacturers, primarily located in Taiwan.
These companies were contract manufacturers for the computer
original equipment manufacturers (OEMs), such as Dell, Compaq,
and Hewlett Packard. Testing and design-in of our products was usually done with the OEM. Shipments of the products went directly to
Taiwan. We nearly took over the thermal solution business for notebook computers, accounting for about one-third of our total sales.

As computing of all types was growing, sales were also generated from desktop computers and servers. As the world of computing grew, the sales of semiconductors grew. We were heavily into the
thermal solution for semiconductor test equipment, not only with
Schlumberger but also Teradyne. We developed an advanced T-putty
that Teradyne used exclusively. The semiconductor test business
became over 25 percent of our total sales. Sales continued to grow
through the year 2000 to nearly $19 million at a rate ranging from
one and a half to two times year over year. Sales were driven by outside manufacturers' representatives (reps) strategically placed around

the world, operating strictly on commission. They were managed by myself, initially, and, ultimately, through inside sales/application engineers, to whom I transferred my technical knowledge. Using commission-only reps was a key step in the whole process and fundamental to our success.

Marketing was historically weak, mainly due to lack of resources. The one major strategy that served Thermagon very well throughout my tenure with the company was to diligently collect all potential customer leads from trade shows, new product release responses, rep referrals, and personally calling them to determine the best product for their application, and then sending them free samples overnight. My competitors personally told me that they could not manage to send out free samples overnight.

Believe me, the good will that free overnight samples created with the customer was tremendous! Conveying that sense of urgency generated significant confidence with the customer. The customer would often call back and say they would like for the product to be thinner, thicker, softer, stickier, etc., and we would respond with a new set of samples sent overnight. Sometimes these requests would require custom formulation, and sometimes these formulations would turn into real products. The motto, "always listen to your customer" proved to be invaluable advice.

It became time to upgrade our product literature from the simple computer-generated versions. We ultimately created one-page glossy-printed pieces for each product family and a separate one-page product selection guide. We created a double-sized print piece for our printed circuit board materials, including a guide for the many configurations that were possible. We published advertisements in most all the electronic-focused technical journals and had several featured articles published as well.

In 1996, a new journal called *Electronics Cooling* was published, which validated the extreme need for thermal management in electronic systems. Thermagon's circuit board material piece became the cover of one of the early editions. Electronics cooling became the buzzwords of the decade.

In this era, web pages and websites became the "must-haves" for most all corporations. We were quick to register our URL for Thermagon.com. Creating our website was an ongoing process. Craig, who became our computer guru, led the work to create and continually improve our site during these growth years. By 2000, we reached out to a marketing firm who helped Thermagon with branding and positioning our website.

During these growth years, we were expanding our product selection through the great work of R&D and searching for new markets. In addition to serving the computer industry, we branched out into telecommunications, military, automotive, audio, memory modules, disc drives, power converters and network systems. By the year 2000, our top 20 customers were generating 80 percent of our revenue. From 1997 to 1999, our inquiries, quotes, and orders increased between 150 to 200 percent. By 2001, after our move into the new building, my eldest son, Jim, a mechanical engineer, would step up to be the sales and marketing leader.

In these growth years, the sales bookings drove all other aspects of the business rather than the business driving sales. In other words, our products were notably superior and in great demand. This phenomenon is very uncommon and could only last for a relatively short time. All products have a limited lifespan and will never remain mainstream indefinitely. Once the world of thermal management in electronics became aware and learned about our products, all competitor's sights were focused on us. The competitors tried every means to determine how I was attaining such high thermal performance. For Thermagon, staying in front technically would be a huge challenge going forward. As my dad would have said, "We must make hay while the sun shines."

Travel became the order of the day. Jim was very busy and needed to manage the growth in production. On-time delivery was imperative, and having planned and organized procedures for manufacturing was a huge responsibility. To accomplish, this required the hiring of many new people, all of whom needed to be trained. Having assumed the marketing responsibility, I was the only likely candidate to travel. Until now, travel was not affordable. Our customers and manufacturer's representatives (reps) were merely names and voices on the other end of a phone to me. As I prepared to begin this travel, I began thinking about all the engineers that I would meet who would be key to specifying the Thermagon materials into their electronic systems. I conjectured that these engineers would prefer to speak with someone technical, as opposed to an administrative type such as the CEO. That led to my decision to have Thermagon business cards printed, naming me as the technical director rather than as the CEO. So I began traveling the world as the technical director of Thermagon.

Off I went to Silicon Valley to meet my rep there for the first time. He was key to the design-in of many materials in the early years. He introduced me to key customers, which led me to better understand their thermal needs. I began to formulate my own relationship with many of the engineers. What I learned was transferred back to our application engineers and R&D staff. Other key areas that I began to visit were Southern California, Texas, Research Triangle Park in North Carolina, and New England. Soon I began to travel internationally with Asia at the top of my list.

My first trip to Asia was in 1996. Traveling alone, I visited Singapore, Taiwan, and Korea. In Singapore, I was met by a representative of Aavid Engineering, a company headquartered in Laconia, New Hampshire, making heat sinks and providing thermal solutions. With their help, I was able to visit Compaq computer, who was beginning to ramp up production of notebook computers in Singapore. As I waited in the foyer of their facility for my appointment, I became a bit nervous and fidgety. I reached into my briefcase and pulled out one of the Thermagon Folders, shiny white with bright blue letters reading, "Thermagon." In it were the computer-generated data sheets—certainly not fancy. In a matter of about two or three minutes, someone walking by spotted that folder and immediately escorted me to a conference room. *Wow!* I thought, *do they really recognize the Thermagon name around here so far from Cleveland?*

The answer was "yes!"

I could have laid that folder down anywhere in the United States, and chances are no one would have noticed. Compaq went on to be a major purchaser of our materials.

I soon realized that Aavid was trying to convince me to give them exclusive rights to selling our materials with their heat sinks. Of course, that was never going to happen. However, saying "no" to Asians did not seem to have the same impact as it does here in the states. They were very reluctant to take "no" for an answer. The Aavid people followed me to Taiwan and were waiting at my hotel when I arrived. I was forced into continuing my explanation as to why I would not give them exclusive rights to my products. Despite their disappointment, Aavid continued to be a customer. They were very commodity oriented and often purchased our lower-end materials.

Despite the interference of Aavid, my main purpose of visiting Taiwan was to meet DJ, my rep, who I had only communicated with a few times on the phone and by fax. E-mail was not yet available. DJ was already generating significant business. We connected immediately. The Asian culture, particularly in Taiwan, was exceedingly energizing to me. They were completely committed to the design-in of our materials into electronics in Asia. They radiated a sense of urgency. They explained that it was imperative that my shipments be on time. One day late, and I needed to write a letter of apology and promise never to be late again. Interesting, I thought. In the United States, a week late would be considered on time. I loved that sense of urgency.

While in Taiwan, one of my employees who had been recently hired to manage our thermally conductive printed circuit board materials arrived to discuss this aspect of our business. The market for these materials was not yet developed, and technical parameters were still in development. I must admit, I welcomed a familiar English-speaking person to connect with, if only for a short time.

One little interesting story happened while in Taiwan one evening when I had some time to myself. I walked into the hotel restaurant, hoping to just relax. However, they seated me in the front near the television. The summer Olympics were on. As part of my effort to relax, I ordered a beer with my meal. No big deal, I thought.

Little did I know that in Asia, beer comes in liter bottles. So in they came with this liter of beer just for me. Oh boy, I rolled my eyes and thought too late now. I stuck out enough just being blond, American, and by myself. Oh well, I was learning. The truth is that no one in that hotel was going to let anything happen to me. One morning when I was waiting for transportation to my appointment, pacing back and forth, letting off my nervous energy, an employee of the hotel came to me and asked if I was okay. Obviously, little went unnoticed.

My experience in Korea was quite different. The reps who were organizing my stay were recommended to me by the World Trade Center in Cleveland. Their connection to the world of electronics was dubious, and they spoke very little English. They usually met me in the hotel for our daily meetings, and we would take public transportation. The food they ordered for me was so spicy that eating it was a challenge. One day, the gentleman lunching with me ordered his normal kimchi and soup for both himself and me. I could barely get it down. He proceeded to explain that this is what he eats every day for lunch and that he would *not* get cancer. I was quick to believe him. Cancer couldn't survive kimchi. The value of the meetings was dubious. I was learning. *Note, do not go to Korea without an interpreter unless your rep speaks fluent English.*

My last night in South Korea, four gentlemen from the rep office took me out to dinner. I was used to the all-male world, so I didn't think much of it. During dinner, one gentleman looked me in the eye and asked, "Why did your company send you?"

"The company is mine. I founded it and invented the products." I smiled broadly. The men were speechless and, obviously, not used to dealing with women in business. My business cards stated that I was the technical director, so they had no reason to believe otherwise.

South Korean society was, and still is, deeply rooted in Confucianism. One particular theme is patriarchy, a system where each gender has its own role in a family. Although the patriarchal culture has undergone changes, as South Korea continues to develop in the modern world, the mentality of gender specific roles seems to remain strong within the society, inherently bearing gender discrimination, particularly in employment. Consequently, employers are more reluctant to hire females, fearing they are more likely to quit working in certain stages in their lives.

South Korea ranks 115th out of 145 countries in providing economic participation and opportunity for women. Women earn nearly 40 percent less than men, which is more than double the average in the Organization for Economic Cooperation and Development (OECD) countries. The thirty-five OECD countries are all democracies operating as free economies. Less than 2 percent of women workers are corporate executives. One can understand why the gentlemen at dinner were curious about my role and why I was representing Thermagon in our meetings. After returning to the United States, I was able to find a new South Korean rep who spoke English and who was active in the world of electronics and able to introduce me into companies like Samsung, etc.

As the business grew, travel became more and more frequent. I hired an international business consultant named Denys. She organized my itinerary for overseas trips and coached me on the business culture for each country. Travel abroad in the early growth years centered mainly around Taiwan with side trips to other Asian countries. By year 2000, Japan, Hong Kong, and China had been added to our destinations. One trip to Japan was particularly noteworthy. Much talk and publicity prevailed about Japanese mastery of copying other companies' technology as opposed to inventing. At this time, Japan was the only country outside the United States who had any significant thermal interface material development and suppliers, most notably Shin-Etsu.

Before making this trip to Japan, Thermagon had agreed to several visits to Thermagon from a company named Intermark. When the Intermark people arrived, several in the group were Japanese. I alerted all employees to be in extra secrecy mode, not to let anyone move about unattended, which was a best practice for us. The company came across as a bit mysterious, and their motive for visiting was never clear. We supplied them with some samples, and they purchased a few bits and pieces of materials, never enough to be part of a commercially viable product. With further investigation, I learned that Intermark was the US name for Kitagawa, a well-known company in Japan. This is much like the current company, Foxconn, being the US arm of the Taiwanese company, Hon Hai, an electronic contract manufacturer operating mostly in China. Foxconn became a significant customer of Thermagon in the early 2000s. Further checking on Kitagawa led us to learn that Kitagawa was the Japanese rep for our major competitor Bergquist. Never would you build a relationship or do business with your competitor's rep. When they first came to visit, they would ask numerous times, "Where da facry? Where da facry?" It was obvious to them that I did not have the typical type of manufacturing process as my competitors.

They recognized that we must be doing something different. We always made it clear to any visitors that viewing the manufacturing was not possible. In addition, everyone had to sign a nondisclosure agreement just to be safe. My rather flip saying was, "If we show you the factory, we must shoot you at the door."

On one of their visits, as we took a restroom break, all departed for the facilities, except one, and he stayed back in my office. He proceeded to make me a proposition.

"If I pay you one million dollars, will you show me the factory?" I turned beet red and told him, in no uncertain terms, that he could not see the factory under any circumstances and that I was tired of repeating the same explanation over and over. I swear my blood pressure has never gone higher. I nicknamed him the "Million Dollar Man." After this experience, we would ask for an agenda and purpose for a meeting before we would consent to meet with them.

As I went off to Japan to organize my own rep network, I added a visit to Kitagawa to my itinerary. I also had convinced Denys, my international consultant, to join me on this trip. Culturally, Japan is probably the hardest to understand. They have a procedure for everything, and Americans will never get it. Where you sit at the conference table, how you hand out your business cards, and on and on. I am quite certain that I was the first woman in the boardroom of many of the multinational Japanese companies I visited. One would never travel to Japan as the technical director, for example. Being the CEO carries much prestige to the Japanese businessperson.

We traveled by train from Tokyo to Nagoya to visit Kitagawa. The Million Dollar Man met us at the train station. The engineer who had visited in the United States was also present at the meeting. The usual roundabout conversations were taking place when I confronted them with their relationship with Bergquist. I questioned their intent to continue to build a relationship with us, considering that they had never made a major purchase. The engineer sat with his hands over his head, as if to say, "We've been busted!" And oh, by the way, it was Mr. Kitagawa Jr. who was chairing the meeting. I suppose, as some kind of a reward for enduring their fallacious behavior, Mr. Kitagawa Jr. invited me to dinner with *the* Mr. Kitagawa, to which I declined. All the persuasion in the world was not going to trick me into falling into that trap.

As politely as I tried to decline their invitation, it was extremely difficult and definitely a cultural "no-no" in Japan. It was obvious to them that I knew that their sole reason for continuing the relationship was to learn my secrets. Fearing that we might have to fend for ourselves to return to the train, the Million Dollar Man drove us the short distance.

Phew!

It was a meeting I will never forget. Despite this experience, I was truly fascinated with Japan and grew to thoroughly enjoy my visits there.

During this same trip, I was invited to give a talk to a group of Japanese women entrepreneurs. I wasn't aware there was such a thing. I was excited to learn. On arrival to the meeting, there were all of four women waiting anxiously for my speech. Also attending was a male interpreter and a room full of other males who totally dominated the meeting. I gave my speech, answered their questions, and joined them for dinner. The women were delightful. I learned that Japanese women find it very difficult to start a business and rarely ever try to combine family life with a career. There were many questions centered around how I managed my personal life with the business. Working women in Japan would most likely be involved in education rather than the world of business.

All in all, it was a fabulous experience!

The major purpose of this trip was to centralize the purchasing of our products in Japan through one rep. My appointments centered around manufacturers reps and potential customers. Most notably was Furukawa and Fujikura, both manufacturers of heat pipe assemblies needing a thermal interface solution. Both are old-line Japanese companies deeply steeped in Japanese tradition. Women were not normal visitors. Both companies were keenly aware of our products and expressed interest in furthering the relationship. We succeeded in communicating to all parties our intent to direct our Japanese business through one rep.

While Europe was not a hotbed for high-end electronics, Thermagon established a presence there and visited once or twice each year. Destinations most common were Germany, France, and the UK. My experience led me to believe that Europe was a great place for a vacation, but not nearly as exciting from a business perspective. That sense of urgency and enthusiasm experienced in Asia did not exist in Europe. Vacations or holidays, as the Europeans called them, were frequent and long.

France, Germany, and the UK were very competitive among themselves and very resistant to collaborating through one common rep. Much of the European business centered around power supplies, locomotive, and communications. They were getting by with the low-end commodity type thermal materials and were reluctant to pay a premium for better performance. We managed several medium-sized accounts as a result of our efforts.

Travel in the United States centered mainly around California, particularly Silicon Valley, Texas, and New England. Even though manufacturing of electronics was gradually moving to Asia, components and materials were still often designed-in through the OEMs in the United States. Examples of these OEMs are Dell, Compaq, Hewlett Packard, Cisco Systems, Silicon Graphics, and Sun Microsystems. Also, we exhibited at three to four trade shows each year, usually in the United States.

The process of reaching out into the world and meeting our customers enhanced Thermagon's visibility and credibility, leading to increased sales. Visiting our customers' facilities around the world was a huge learning opportunity and gave us insight into our customers' future needs for thermally conductive materials. Our learnings could be transferred back to R&D and became the basis for our future new products.

CHAPTER SIXTEEN

THE NUTS AND BOLTS

Creating functional, yet beautifully colorful workspace adorned with art will energize employees and improve productivity.

I n order to keep up with our rapidly growing sales, Thermagon needed to dramatically expand its manufacturing capability and physical plant. On the surface, it might appear that this process should be straightforward. Having noted that many start-ups lose their business because they are unable to cost-effectively manufacture products in sufficient volume. I understood that this production scale-up was incredibly vital. Issues like missing shipment dates, securing raw material supply, losing critical product properties, and sufficient cash flow for expansion needed to be quickly and adequately addressed. Jim was responsible for effectively expanding our manufacturing capabilities.

For those of us whose background is in research and development, scaling up a process to high volume and attempting to automate wherever possible often results in a loss of key properties. Most important for us would be the thermal conductivity. Our process was definitely a batch process, but parts of it could be streamlined to increase efficiency and shorten time. Jim, Craig, production workers, and R&D employees worked together to ensure that the process was optimized to achieve maximum thermal conductivity. Certain steps in the process needed to be carefully timed. Certain temperatures needed to be maintained, and many equipment parameters could not be compromised. Even so, we were able to develop the process to a larger scale and reduce production times and still maintain the properties of the products and be cost effective.

The process for manufacturing the Thermagon products consisted of three main functions. First came the mixing, which required a specific type of mixing equipment with careful time monitoring and sometimes requiring heat. Then came the forming of the mixture into sheets using rolling equipment that was custom-made to meet our needs. Sheets were formed in thicknesses ranging from 0.005 inches to sometimes as thick as 0.200 inches. The variation of thickness across a sheet needed to be carefully monitored, since thermal resistance through the sheet was proportional to thickness. Finally, the sheets needed to be cured using either ovens or laminating presses.

Missing shipment dates was never an option. "Just in time" (JIT) were the buzzwords of the day. Electronic equipment manufacturers would never tolerate our holding up their production line by late shipments, particularly in Asia. Missing shipments dates could have seriously jeopardized our success. One day, as we were feverishly working long hours to keep up with the orders, a gentleman from Inventec arrived at our plant unannounced. Inventec was the contract manufacturer for Compaq notebook computers in Taiwan. Inventec had placed a significant order the week before. The gentleman had flown from Taipei to Cleveland to wait for their order to be completed, so he could hand carry the parts back to Taipei. As fate would have it, my great employees had worked over the weekend to complete their order. When this gentleman arrived, all we needed to do was to package the shipment and hand it over to him. He was back in Taiwan with parts in less than forty-eight hours. Wow! Was he impressed. We had just acquired a loyal customer for many years to come.

As our sales increased, Thermagon invested heavily in capital equipment to make this happen. Fortunately, the profitability of Thermagon was adequate to fund the needed expansion both in equipment and space. Starting in 1996 until 1999, Thermagon spent about $1.5 million on capital equipment and renovation of leased space in the building on West Twenty-Fifth Street. Luckily, we were able to expand from seven thousand square feet to about twenty thousand square feet at this West Twenty-Fifth Street location. This expenditure included laboratory and office space, as well as equipment and space for both machines and production. Additionally, we added a second shift to help meet our production demands. Parking then became one of our major issues.

In 1999, we began the process of looking for additional space. The existing owner of our building on West Twenty-Fifth Street considered selling at about three times the appraised value of the building. Still, we would need to solve the parking problem. That consideration was abandoned. After looking at several other possibilities, we found a building on Detroit Avenue at Forty-Fifth Street. It was two buildings put together. The old section was from the early twentieth century while the newer portion was from the 1970s. It had about fifty thousand square feet, was located on the near west side of Cleveland, and was priced fairly. We purchased the building for $535,000 from our earnings and subsequently put $3 million in renovation, equipment, and furnishings. To finance this portion, we used a line of credit with National City Bank, and when the project was finished, we turned the remaining debt into a term loan. This was the first and only time Thermagon incurred debt.

The old brick section had beautiful curved windows and made excellent space for our administration functions on the third floor and the laboratory, conference room, and additional offices on the first floor. The second floor was reserved for expansion. We replaced every window, pipe and wire in the building, and put hard wood floors down in the old building. The newer section was used for production. Jim took on the task of managing this project. My daughter Diane had recently returned from California touting her skills as a budding artist. We contracted with her to provide very colorful contemporary paintings to hang on the walls. In the first quarter of 2000, we moved in. It was magnificent! Jim had done a fantastic job. Included was a handmade cherry desk for me that was made by a carpenter in the West Twenty-Fifth Street building. Several months after moving we hosted an open-house and art exhibition to showcase our new digs to the community and to jumpstart Diane's art venture.

As our volumes increased, obtaining sufficient boron nitride to meet our specifications became a concern. Boron Nitride was a critical ingredient in our products. Despite our efforts to specify boron nitride powders from more than one supplier, the powder in our fastest-growing product could only be sourced from Carborundum.

When British Petroleum sold Carborundum to Saint-Gobain in 1995, I had developed a relationship with the director of Carborundum who had just recently retired. Not only were we paying very high prices for our powder, we needed to be guaranteed an adequate supply. This retiree shared with me some general insights into the cost barriers of the powder and the size of the overall business. Estimating that the boron nitride portion of Carborundum was about $12 million in revenue, I theorized that Saint-Gobain probably did not purchase Carborundum for this small piece. After several discussions with my advisors, particularly Paul, I decided to put together a group that would approach Saint-Gobain with the proposal to purchase the boron nitride business.

Vertically integrating Thermagon to include the boron nitride business could make sense and guarantee our continued supply. So off we went to New York City to meet a Saint-Gobain executive from France to discuss our idea. Saint-Gobain made their position very clear. They were not interested in selling the boron nitride business. Instead of divesting of the boron nitride business, they proposed providing Thermagon with a supply agreement that would guarantee our needed supply and allow for price breaks based on volume. We spent the next several months negotiating the details. The solution was a sensible one for both parties. I was elated to get the price per pound of BN down from the original $92 to under $50, depending on volume. Thermagon became arguably the largest purchaser of BN in the world, which led to the building of a new BN plant at Carborundum/Saint-Gobain. Having the courage to pursue the purchase of the BN business from Saint-Gobain led to a negotiation that provided a win-win solution for both of our needs. Thermagon received a more affordable, guaranteed supply of BN that met our specifications, and Saint-Gobain increased their sales and profits. Additionally, now that Carborundum had become a legitimate subsidiary of Saint-Gobain, the probability of BP filing a lawsuit against Thermagon became very low.

CHAPTER SEVENTEEN

ONE BIG HAPPY FAMILY

*Treating employees with respect and dignity
reaps unbelievable rewards.*

All the while that sales were growing, that markets were extending across the globe, that travel was increasing, and our physical plant and capabilities were expanding, Thermagon was frantically recruiting new people to join our company. Thermagon had seven employees to start 1996, and by the end of 2000, we had grown to 120. Those seven employees included myself, my two sons, two production people, one testing/research and development person, and a circuit board material manager. We all wore many hats. Generally speaking, Jim managed the production/operation side of things. Craig managed the administration and IT. And I managed the sales, marketing, research and development.

In 1996, we first addressed the need for production workers. We found success acting on recommendations from existing employees and through our relationship with WIRE-NET (Western Industrial Retention Network), a nonprofit organization dedicated to improving the community through nurturing manufacturing and the jobs and prosperity that come with it. For Thermagon, they screened potential production candidates and sent them our way for final approval.

We also learned that our recommendations from existing employees were generally quite good. These employees did not want to be embarrassed by recommending someone who was not honest, ethical, and a good worker. Our production workers were hired from the inner-city neighborhood in which we resided.

Not by design, it so happened that the eleven production workers employed in 1996 were primarily Hispanic women. These were untrained people, who mostly had never worked before or were previously on welfare. We made one of the original production workers the production supervisor. This supervisor devised a method for selecting these employees based on basic arithmetic skills, personal values, and potential work ethic. Their employment was temporary/probationary for the first three months, and then as they demonstrated their work skills, we made them bona fide employees. We took pride in our training and nurturing of these employees.

I personally believed that it was of the utmost importance to treat our employees as human beings rather than as human resources. The reward came back to Thermagon a hundred times over. Seldom did we lose an employee. All employees were part of the Thermagon family. The only other hire of 1996 was an inside sales and application engineer. My ability to transfer my knowledge and rapport with our customers over to him was critical to the success of Thermagon. Again, in 1997, we added another thirteen employees, mostly for production and with similar demographics and diversity. One exception was a chemistry graduate from Baldwin Wallace University, Jason, who joined me in research and development.

One day, Jason and one of our other recent hires came to me with a question. They were in the process of ordering business cards and wanted to know what they should use as their title. I looked at them quizzically and responded, "Whatever you want."

They were speechless, as they trundled off shaking their heads, left with the decision of what label they should include on their business cards. I've always chose to place little emphasis on labels and titles. What is really important is what you contribute and what you stand for in life.

Jason's growth at Thermagon is one of the many stories demonstrating how Thermagon was able to change lives. Jason grew up in Ashtabula, Ohio, and worked his way through college to attain his degree. As a first-generation college graduate in his family, he appeared to be an anomaly. Nurturing, support, and encouragement did not seem present in abundance during his youth. Jason was smart, creative, and eager to succeed, just what Thermagon needed. His bachelor's degree in chemistry from a liberal arts college was similar to my educational background. It wasn't long until he was making an impact on product and process development. He was a little weak on soft skills, but a little nurturing and time would hopefully improve his personal relationships.

As I worked with Jason, he revealed a few stories that confirmed my analysis. One day, I told Jason I needed him to travel to Long Island to evaluate some mixing equipment, when he replied, "Oh, but I have never been on an airplane," to which I replied, "You are about to have the experience."

On another day, Jason shared that he had used part of his bonus money to buy his grandfather a television. Like most people, I assumed that nearly all households had televisions. Wrong! Jason continued to develop as a strong member of our technical team. Even though I saw the potential, our technical director hired in 1999 made the most impact on Jason's career at Thermagon. So much so that when he retired in 2015, Jason replaced him as the new technical director.

In 1998, we hired twenty more people of which about half were for production. The other half included roles such as a general manager, two inside sales and application engineers; an engineering support person, three for research and development; and additional administrative people, including an administrative assistant for me. All played vital roles in our successful growth. Thermagon ended the year with about fifty-two employees.

Finally, in 1999, we added significant professional help to our team that included managers in quality, maintenance, finance, and a technical director, Rich, to manage research and development. He came from Advanced Ceramics, one of our two boron nitride suppliers. Rich left Advanced Ceramics in 1998 to finish his PhD. I kept in close contact with him during those months with the hope and intention of hiring him for Thermagon when his PhD work was complete. My effort paid off. Rich was key to our future success. The remaining employees of the thirty we hired were in either production, technical support, or administration.

After our move into the Detroit Avenue building in the first quarter of 2000, Jim moved from operations to manage sales and marketing. A couple of years later, we hired a sales manager. With that change, we moved Craig into operations. The organization chart was now built out to look like a real company. We added about twenty-five more employees and an additional thirteen contract people to produce our nearly $19 million in sales revenue in 2000. It was a banner year!

You must be wondering after all these additions, "Where is the human resources manager?" That is a good question, I might add. Of all the functions in the company, this is the one that I struggled with the most. I had attended many "best practices" talks, and I had Paul as an adviser so that I knew the role was extremely important.

I was known to say that the role was like a balloon up in the air. Whoever catches it gets the job. Fortunately, a woman in production came to me and said she was interested in assuming the role. She caught the proverbial "balloon." She began learning the role and soon asked about attending college at night. She received her degree from Baldwin Wallace University in human resources, which Thermagon paid for. She is a human resource professional to this day. She is one of the many Thermagon success stories exemplifying Thermagon's role in changing people's lives.

Thermagon's goal was to improve every employee's skills and quality of life in the years that they spent with us. Parents were allowed to take time off to tend to their children when the inevitable problems of child-rearing occurred. An open-door policy and a suggestion box were established to ensure that all employees had access to management. It was not unusual for any number of the employees to rally together when one of their colleagues was in need of a helping hand. A group of employees, myself included, helped a newly hired Hispanic girl, also new to Cleveland, find a place to live. We helped to paint and clean up the place before she moved in.

To further reinforce this notion of a respectful work culture, Thermagon used an environmentally safe manufacturing process and provided a clean, attractive, and temperature-controlled work environment, complete with original contemporary paintings from Diane Latham. Most manufacturing environments did not have these amenities. Thermagon also offered a 401(k) plan and health benefits.

To complement our current caring culture, Thermagon instituted the following programs, intended to share our financial success and demonstrate our appreciation for the dedication of all employees.

The Bonus Program: Once the Thermagon sales took off, and we started generating a significant profit, the Latham family wanted to share the wealth with all the employees. Despite the large increase in employees, the large capital investment for both office and manufacturing equipment, renovation, and ultimately the purchase of our new building, Thermagon generated net profits of between 25 and 35 percent of revenue. Each year, we set aside 5 to 8 percent of our profit and gave each employee a generous bonus in December. My son Jim devised the method for distributing the money.

The pot of money set aside for bonuses was divided into three tranches. The first took 50 percent of the money and divided it according to each person's pay scale. The second took 25 percent of the money and divided it according to seniority. The third tranche took the last 25 percent of the money and divided it according to merit. Every employee received a bonus, except for myself. The size of the bonuses was notable. Rarely would the bonus be less than a thousand dollars and would range upward to between five and ten thousand dollars. Our employees were immensely grateful, particularly the factory workers. What a blessing it was for me to share the rewards. At Christmastime, I would dress in my red plaid skirt and Santa hat and pass out the checks.

Continuing Education Program: Thermagon hired their production employees primarily from the surrounding neighborhood on the near west side of Cleveland. That resulted in employees who were mostly female and of Hispanic descent. The level of English competency varied widely. Many had never held a job before. The skill level was relatively low. However, the work ethic and willingness to learn was obvious. Consequently, our staff reflected on how they could impact their skills. They came up with the idea to have classes at Thermagon during work hours to teach relevant skills. The company contacted the Cleveland school system and asked if they could provide teachers who could fill this gap. The answer was yes. We began to provide classes in English as a second language, math skills, and computer skills. In addition, we provided opportunities to attend classes off-site, either at WIRENET or at the Old Stone Foundation Wise program in soft skills. Skills learned included phone etiquette and work-related communications. Thermagon was serious about enhancing one's quality of life as a result of their work experience with us.

College Tuition Reimbursement Program: For those of our employees who sought furthering their education in a more formal way, Thermagon provided assistance in obtaining a college degree. I previously referenced our human resources manager who attended college to hone her skills for this profession. However, for the employees, in general, I would reimburse them for any courses that were part of a legitimate college degree program. The courses did not need to have a direct correlation to the needs of Thermagon. The level of reimbursement was related to the grade received in each course. Those who took advantage of this offer have been forever grateful.

There were other unique perks that our employees experienced. Thermagon held monthly meetings with the entire staff to keep them up to date on the current status of the business, including reports on new products developed, sales forecasts, changes to any procedures, company profitability, etc. The employees were well-informed as to the health of the company.

Most important, they were included, and our status was transparent. Even though the impact of these meetings was nearly impossible to quantify, I believe that the sharing of information led to a more conscientious workforce, better positive energy and morale, and increased productivity.

One other perk that I personally provided employees was a personal lunch with me during their birthday month. We would convene in our conference room, and I provided a catered lunch with party hats and whistles. It was a great way to get to know everyone and listen to their stories and perceptions of Thermagon.

For me, it was one thing to have my technology successful in the marketplace and to experience such sales growth but to have the opportunity to enhance the quality of so many people's lives was truly what I call the "frosting on the cake."

CHAPTER EIGHTEEN

RESEARCH AND DEVELOPMENT

Don't ever say it can't be done.

I considered research and development as the heart of the company. It is the generator that makes all other functions of the company relevant and function with purpose. The technology for creating high thermal conductivity polymer-based materials, capable of being manufactured cost effectively, coupled with the forethought that heat was destined to be a critical issue in computing as systems ramped up in power and functionality while continuing to miniaturize, drove the success of the business. Computing was evolving at a very rapid rate in the nineties. Products could go in or out of favor very quickly based on the evolving heat management needs.

For example, a thermal material supplier could be designed into or out of a notebook computer every nine months. Staying relevant with state-of-the-art products was the task of research and development. We were continually improving and creating new products. Additionally, research and development worked with production to assure each product could be manufactured effectively with little impact on the critical properties. I personally managed the research and development function until 1999 when I hired Rich as technical director.

Always attempting to achieve the lowest thermal resistance for a given application, the Thermagon research and development staff was continually introducing new products. We started in 1996 with about six families of materials and introduced another eight to ten additional product families during the growth years. Generally speaking, research and development was either balancing thermal conductivity with softness, elasticity, and compressibility for filling a gap usually larger than forty mils, or they were balancing thickness with flowability for very thin interfaces usually ten mils or less.

T-pli, the material Intel designed into notebooks, used mostly in either ten or twenty mil thicknesses, had high thermal conductivity and relative softness compared to competitive products. T-pli was our number one seller in these growth years.

In addition to the several gap fillers introduced by research and development, phase-change materials became a focus. Using polymer-based phase-change materials that would flow when the CPU or other electronic devices heated up became a significant part of our development work. To flow was great for thermal resistance because as the material became liquid it would fill all the small imperfections on the surface of the heat sink and device, replacing the insulating air. Rich and his team received ten patents for their work in phase-change materials. Additional work for thin flowable interfaces focused on thermal greases.

The thermally conductive adhesive films developed by Thermagon became the basis for our circuit board designs. In addition to high thermal conductivity, these epoxy-based films are solid and free standing at room temperature, very thin (.005 inches), very even in thickness, good adhesives, and have high dielectric strength. There were no other adhesive films comparable to these on the market. These films allowed us to build laminates with circuitry built on heat-spreading metal bases or cores for maximum heat transfer. Two competitors had introduced thermally conductive circuit board laminates but used a totally differed approach with lower thermal performance. Maximizing the performance of these laminates was a major thrust of the research and development effort.

Characterizing the Thermagon products by performing a multitude of tests was also the function of research and development. Some tests were so specialized that no off-the-shelf equipment was available, forcing us to design and make testing devices ourselves. Thermagon could not always afford the needed test equipment, or the frequency of need did not justify the expense so that we sometimes paid to have the tests run in an outside laboratory.

As if this wasn't enough, new products needed to be developed in months, not years. In such a fast-moving industry, research and development did not have the luxury of ample time. Either the researcher believed he/she could find success in the months allotted or best not to start at all. Oh, and please never tell me "it cannot be done."

CHAPTER NINETEEN

TIME TO ORGANIZE

*Not only the investors incurred risks but
also early Thermagon employees.*

During these high growth-rate years of Thermagon, managing the quotes, purchase orders, the supply chain, production schedule, billing, accounts receivable, etc. became a major endeavor. In came Craig to the rescue. The simple database program he set up to run the company in 1995 was no longer adequate for the task at hand. After consulting with many experts, Craig purchased and implemented an enterprise resource planning (ERP) business software package called Symix. Symix offered a suite of applications called Syteline. Thermagon began the implementation process in March of 1998 and successfully went live with the package in April of 1999. This software package was a significant investment for Thermagon of about $100,000. The package itself cost $50,000, and another $50,000 was needed for implementation and consulting. Syteline provided Thermagon with many new capabilities. This software acted as the business framework that integrated manufacturing and finance throughout the entire order process. The many tools included financial management, inventory control, job costing/product costing, supply chain management, production and capacity planning, etc. These many functions improved customer service, reduced operating costs, minimized returns and rework, and created an ability to measure performance. In addition, Syteline provided real-time financial and production information, helpful for strategic executive decisions.

During these growth years, Paul, my mentor from Arthur Anderson / Price Waterhouse Coopers, became active as a strategist for Thermagon. In 1996, he implemented many tax credits and savings for Thermagon:

Manufacturing tax credit	About 13.5 percent over seven years
Research tax credit	Worth $6,000
State jobs credit	About 55 percent for seven years on new jobs created over the next three years with our promise of thirty jobs
City tax abatement	About 60 percent on new personal property, new inventory, and leasehold improvements for seven years
Export tax credit	Quite unique. We had zero imports and significant exports

Paul also helped me with succession planning, devising a plan for transferring ownership of half of my shares to my two sons, Jim and Craig. He arranged for an evaluation of Thermagon to determine its value. Through the use of ESBTs (electing small business trusts), ownership of half my shares were transferred to my sons with minimal tax liability.

During this time, Paul and my attorney, Rob, from Baker & Hostettler, split the Thermagon shares from the original issued 303 shares to 15,150 shares, including the 303 voting shares. The authorized shares of 750 were split to 30,300 shares. There was no dilution of ownership to shareholders in this process.

Since Thermagon was an S Corporation, all their earnings flowed through the individual shareholders' personal income tax returns. Thermagon's net earnings were significant, 25 to 35 percent of revenue. Shareholders, including myself, would not have cash on hand to cover this tax liability. Again, Paul was instrumental in helping me determine the amount of the shareholder's distribution, payable quarterly. Assuming the shareholders were in the highest tax bracket, approximately 50 percent of earnings was paid out to the shareholders each year to cover their tax debt. As you may recall, Thermagon still had ample revenue to cover their exploding growth.

Thermagon formed a board of directors consisting of, ultimately, myself and my two sons. To provide corporate governess, I developed an advisory board consisting of the three directors and five other professionals, representing the disciplines of finance, legal, manufacturing, technical, and marketing. All, but one, came from the Cleveland business community. The other, the technical expert, came from the electronics packaging industry as a consultant. We had several meetings intending to learn and hopefully receive a critique of our process in each of the disciplines. The time and energy required of me to plan and manage these meetings never seemed proportional to the benefit received. Shame on me! Ultimately, the group finally just faded away.

The challenge in managing such explosive growth was to remain prudent in evaluating our capital and manpower needs. I needed to manage the compensation of our newly acquired management team to be competitive. Also, I needed to determine the fair and adequate pay for our staff and production workers. We now had a nearly complete organization chart with a CEO, general manager, finance manager, production manager, technical director, quality director, and a sales and marketing director. My goal was to ultimately have separate sales and marketing directors. Thermagon had now reached the stage where all requests for expenditures were not a complete necessity for the operations of the company. Determining the return on investment became imperative. Looking like a real and successful company now? I think so!

CHAPTER TWENTY

CAN YOU BELIEVE THE INTEREST?

Make sure all business deals are win-win.

Obviously, I was not the only one to think that Thermagon had become a successful company. Many companies contacted us with interest to purchase Thermagon. All would be considered strategic buyers. My response was always the same, "The company is not for sale." Nevertheless, I was always willing to entertain a discussion about why purchasing Thermagon interested them.

I learned a lot with each discussion. For instance, how they envisioned a strategic fit, how they would integrate Thermagon into their culture, how autonomous they would allow Thermagon to operate, did they have experience in making acquisitions, did they fully understand our value proposition, did they have the means to grow the company.

Sometimes I could get a feel for their perception of the value of Thermagon. Most suitors would end the discussion with the hopes that I would contact them in the event that I decided to sell. Whenever possible, I would include Jim and Craig in the discussions, along with Paul for the financial perspective and Rob for legal. Otherwise, these discussions were not shared with any of the employees and were kept top secret. Having the employees speculating that the company might be acquired would have a very negative impact on the morale of the company. My sons were generally noncommittal concerning their interest in selling. To be sure, I think they had mixed feelings. Usually they would answer, "It's your decision, Mom."

The list of suitors included multinational Fortune 500 companies, some had been acquired themselves and operated under a different name and some were midsize companies under a billion dollars in revenue. The larger companies would fly me in their private jets to meet with them at their headquarters.

The list looked like this:

Parker Chomerics	Competitor and EMI Shielding material supplier.
Allied Signal	Merged with Honeywell.
Henkel Loctite	Adhesive supplier, recently, purchased Bergquist, a major competitor.
ICI	Chemical company purchased by Akzo Nobel.
3M	Technology company supplying varied products from adhesives to abrasives.
Isola	Printed circuit board laminate supplier.
Aavid Engineering	Thermal solutions provider, heat sinks, etc. Merged with Thermalloy.
GE	Purchased Advanced Ceramics and now a supplier of silicone and BN. Both are raw materials of Thermagon.
Lubrizol	Chemical company in Cleveland
Laird Technologies	EMI shielding supplier. Customer overlap with thermal materials.
Dow Chemical	Silicone provider, interested in thermal materials. Merged with Dupont.

CHAPTER TWENTY-ONE

THE WORLD IS WATCHING

You cannot be savvy about everything, so always remain humble.

In 1996, recognition of Thermagon was established within the thermal management industry through our updated literature, presentations of white papers at technical symposiums, new product releases, and paid advertisements in trade journals. Also, our products were featured on the cover of trade journals. Our competitors certainly were aware of the Thermagon presence in the thermal management space, and hopefully, potential customers were becoming more aware as well.

By the spring of 1997, Thermagon had peaked the interest of Thomas Petzinger Jr., a writer for the *Wall Street Journal* who published a column called "The Front Lines" each week. As I recall, one of my newly acquired employees spotted one of Petzinger's columns in the *Journal* about a Cleveland company called Bearings Inc. He called Petzinger and enticed him to consider writing about Thermagon with a somewhat "David and Goliath" approach. Lo and behold, Petzinger called back to set up an appointment. Tom and I hit it off instantly. Somehow, he even understood my struggles with British Petroleum. Before long, he had published an article about Thermagon in his "The Front Lines" column of the *Wall Street Journal*. The article titled "Carol Latham Knows the Spoils Go to Those Who Cross Boundaries" touted our success in spite of the unlikely events and combinations that prevailed in my journey. It wasn't long until Tom Petzinger was busy writing a book about a new dynamic generation of innovators and entrepreneurs who were busy creating a collaborative new workplace, a value-added marketplace, and an economy overflowing with opportunity. In his book titled *The New Pioneers—The Men and Women Who are Transforming the Workplace and Marketplace*, I was one of the pioneers he talked about. As Tom put it, my niche or role was turning low-value commodity chemicals into a high-value substance that would improve the performance of electronic equipment. In 1776, Adam Smith wrote that the march of technology requires people capable of combining together the powers of the most distant and dissimilar objects. Tom Petzinger's affirmation of my effort and business were very rewarding and inspiring. To top things off, Tom invited me to the *Wall Street Journal* Millennium Forum called "The Evolution of Commerce at Harvard Business School." This Millennium Forum was a partnership between Microsoft, Harvard Business School, the *Wall Street Journal*, CNBC, and Forrester Research and was created to give CEOs the opportunity to discuss critical business issues that confront all companies as they move forward.

It was 1999, the time of the evolution of commerce but also the evolution of the internet, the evolution of the World Wide Web, and the evolution of global business. I was honored to be a part of it and to have the opportunity to meet people like Steve Ballmer of Microsoft, Brian Williams of CNBC, Tim Burners-Lee (director of the World Wide Web Consortium), Ray Kurzweil (author of *The Age of Intellectual Machines*), and Michael Porter of Harvard Business School. With Michael Porter, this became the beginning of many encounters I had with him involving his creation of the Initiative for a Competitive Inner City (ICIC).

Starting in 1997, further recognition came from Enterprise Development Inc. (EDI), a cooperative nonprofit subsidiary of Case Western Reserve University (CWRU) and Weatherhead School of Management. EDI focuses on businesses with high-growth potential and presents conferences and courses on marketing, leadership, and financing. In addition, EDI created the EDI Innovation Awards to recognize innovation in the region. Thermagon was the recipient of these awards three years in a row. First, for our overall technology for creating high thermal conductivity polymer-based materials. Second, for translating that into high heat transfer printed circuit board designs. And third, for our development of phase-change materials for heat management in electronic systems.

EDI, in conjunction with Weatherhead School of Management, also compiled the "Weatherhead 100," a compilation of the one hundred fastest growing companies in northeast Ohio based on revenue over five years. To qualify, revenue must be more than $100,000 in the first year and over $1 million in the fifth year. In 1998, Thermagon earned the number one ranking in companies with less than $5 million in revenue. Overall, Thermagon ranked third. The following is a table that shows the Thermagon data that qualified them for ranking on the "Weatherhead 100" for the four years they qualified.

Weatherhead 100 Ranking Data

Five Year	Revenue $	% Growth	Employees	% Growth	Year	Ranking
1993-1997	179K–4.9M	2602	3-32	970	1998	3
1994-1998	366K–7.9M	2050	5-49	920	1999	5
1995-1999	645K–11.2M	1638	8-73	813	2000	6
1996-2000	2.2M–18.7M	746	15-121	717	2001	11

Recognition from local business and academic institutions, organizations, and publications were received with great pride, both from myself and the company and its employees. However, Thermagon had no customers in greater Cleveland nor in the entire state of Ohio. Therefore, one should understand that myself and Thermagon took even greater pride in the recognition we received nationally. Similar to the format for the Weatherhead 100, *Inc. Magazine*, a national publication, created a list of the fastest growing private companies called the *Inc. 500*. Thermagon placed on this list of fastest growing companies in the country three years in succession. Most companies rarely make the list more than once. Maintaining such an extraordinary growth is not easy. Thermagon ranked on the list as follows: 1999—96th; 2000—142nd; and 2001—385th.

I often wished that organizations would rank companies based on profit rather than revenue. Because, after all, why are we in business, if it is not to make money?

The *Inc. 500* list did give some recognition, not by ranking but by categorizing the profit level from greater than 16 percent to a profit loss with letter designations of A through F. Thermagon received an "A" rating for both 1999 and 2000. Curiosity made me check how many of the *Inc. 500* companies listed had attained that feat and, to no surprise, it was only 5 percent.

In 1998, the Initiative for a Competitive Inner City (ICIC) and *Inc. Magazine* partnered to create the *Inc. Inner-City 100*, a list of the one hundred companies located in the inner city with the largest growth in revenue. The inner city was then becoming a new frontier of business growth and entrepreneurship. ICIC was succeeding in its mission to transforming thinking about the inner city, its economic potential, and new approaches to economic renewal. These *Inner-City 100* entrepreneurs demonstrate that the inner city offers a compelling opportunity to build and grow businesses by meeting the demands of new markets, tapping new labor forces, and becoming front-runners in the new economy. Thermagon certainly took advantage of tapping a new labor force.

The *Inner-City 100*, representing many industries, had created close to five thousand new jobs in the last five years. They succeeded, not in spite of their location but at least in part because of it. They have seen an opportunity overlooked by others and run with it. Michael Porter of Harvard Business School is the brain child of this movement. In chapter 11 of his book *On Competition*, he describes a new model based on location and business development whereby the inner city enjoys a competitive advantage and creates a niche that is hard to replicate elsewhere. Thermagon became a perfect example of such an inner-city company. Thermagon was placed on this list four years running in the top 20 companies. From the first annual

Inner-city Entrepreneurship Awards Dinner in 1999 through 2002, Thermagon ranked as follows: sixth, seventh, eighth, and sixteenth.

In May of 1999, Mike Hofman wrote about me in a feature article in *Inc. Magazine* titled "Local Area Network." The tagline stated, "Having chosen to build her business far from the high-tech community, Carol Latham proved she could master the one resource that mattered most: other people." In October 2001, Susan Hansen wrote a feature article about my escape from British Petroleum in *Inc. Magazine*. All these national connections through *Inc. Magazine* and the *Inc. 500* and the *Inc. Inner-City 100* served as credibility and validation of the Thermagon business and an educational experience for me, personally.

The Entrepreneur of the Year Program, founded by Ernst & Young, recognizes people who, through ingenuity, daring, hard work, and perseverance, create and build successful businesses. Furthermore, it seeks to promote the importance of entrepreneurship by teaching it as an art and science and by educating the public about its power to transform lives, organizations, and the economy. In 1997 and 1998, I was chosen as a finalist for this program in northeast Ohio. In 1998, I was chosen as a winner in the "Emerging Entrepreneur" category. Again, this recognition gave me the opportunity to attend the Ernst & Young Entrepreneur of the Year International Conference and provide international exposure for Thermagon and a fabulous learning experience for me.

The setting was Palm Springs. The conference featured current Ernst & Young Entrepreneur of the Year recipients, discussing their business successes and problems in candid discussions with other business owners. The national winner in the Emerging Entrepreneur category was Ciena Corporation, a company who later became a customer of Thermagon. The program over several days provided outstanding speakers and workshops designed to meet the needs of the owner-managers of entrepreneurial companies.

My major takeaway from the conference was from a speaker named Harry S. Dent Jr., author of *The Great Boom Ahead*, *Job Shock: Four New Principles Transforming our Work and Space*, and *The Roaring 2000s*. Harry Dent has consulted at the highest levels of business strategy for Fortune 100 companies. His mission is simple: "Helping people understand change."

Remembering that this is 1998, Dent said that by 2006–2008, we should be prepared to make major shifts in our long-term portfolio and asset allocation. I translated that into the need for me to make a decision about cashing out of Thermagon by that general time frame. I believed that timing was very important. I capped off my involvement with the Entrepreneur of the Year program by serving as a judge in 2000 and attending the conference in Palm Springs one more time.

As I managed Thermagon to the best of my ability, it was never my focus to seek or receive recognition or awards. How could this be happening? The many accolades that came my way were overwhelming, yet impossible to refuse. The list goes on:

1998	➤ Recognized by National Association of Women Business Owners ➤ "Rainmaker of the Year" by *Northern Ohio Live* for skill in being able to bring business through the door.
1999	➤ Manny Award for excellence in manufacturing ➤ Inducted into the Ohio Women's Hall of Fame ➤ Governor's E Award for excellence in exporting ➤ Governor Taft recognition of small manufacturing, National Conference of State Legislators
2000	➤ Business Woman of the Year by *Inside Business* ➤ Northeast Ohio (NEO) success award from *Inside Business*—1999 to 2002 ➤ Blue Cross and Blue Shield Innovation in Business Award ➤ George S. Dively Award for Leadership in Neighborhood Development
2002	➤ YWCA The Eleanor Sutler Equality Award for racial and gender equality in the workforce

While I'm on the subject of my ancillary activities that transpired through these years, as I was primarily focused on nurturing and guiding Thermagon to achieve business success, I should include the many speeches that I gave to many business organizations, rotary clubs and universities throughout the region.

I found this work to be especially rewarding with the hope that someone in the audience would be inspired to step out of their comfort zone and become an entrepreneur. I truly believed that if I could do it with multiple odds stacked against me, certainly one of those in the audience could also make a success of being an entrepreneur.

As a member of Vistage, formerly called Tech, the opportunity to improve my effectiveness became real. As an international organization, Vistage has solidified its reputation as the world's most trusted executive coaching organization. Vistage brings together peer groups of executives from noncompeting industries who work together with a facilitator to solve the groups' individual problems. Their work is backed by one-to-one coaching from the facilitator and has driven the members to outperform their competition through boom markets and recession. This group of CEOs served as my advisory board for many years.

CHAPTER TWENTY-TWO

WOULD YOU BELIEVE WHO ELSE IS WATCHING?

Surround yourself with talented advisers.

As Thermagon moved into the twenty-first century, ending the year 2000 with close to $19 million in revenue, a competent management team, a dedicated and reliable workforce, continued innovation through research and development, an attractive and functional workplace, and quality computer systems that were state of the art, it could legitimately consider itself a bona fide company—the real McCoy! However, before moving on, one more major "happening" became part of our history.

Again, the mystery centers around the person on the other end of the phone. It is fall 2000, a Friday afternoon capping off a busy workweek at Thermagon, when unbeknownst to me someone has been calling for me several times throughout the day. My executive assistant, Edna, who was very efficient, yet sometimes overprotective had been putting off these calls all day with the belief that they were soliciting money. Some of my friends considered Edna the "Phone Gestapo," for she certainly was conscientious. Well, it was after five o'clock on a Friday afternoon when Edna knocks on my door and says, "I think you need to take this call." It was someone I did not know, someone claiming to be from Austin, Texas, and part of the George W. Bush campaign for president of the United States.

Whoopee!

They said they needed to be able to communicate with me over the weekend and arrive at Thermagon on Monday because George W. Bush was planning a visit the following Thursday. I did not believe them. I thought it was a hoax.

"No. No. No," the person on the other end of the line exclaimed. "My information states that we are coming to Cleveland with one stop...Thermagon."

"Are you sure?" I responded.

This person finally convinced me that this was all for real, and believe me, I had no idea what was about to happen. I was busy running a young company. Politics was the furthest thing from my mind.

After a few phone calls over the weekend, people started arriving on Monday from both the Bush campaign team and the secret service. First, they needed to size up our space and determine the logistics on how they could keep George W. safe and still have enough space for him to deliver a major speech. The second floor of our new building was left unfinished and available for future expansion. It was perfect to stage their meeting!

George W.'s team covered the windows and brought in their props. This was advertised as a campaign visit to the middle class. The sign that they posted was titled "Governor Bush's Blueprint for the Middle Class." On the Podium was a sign that read, "Real Plans for Real People."

"And, of course, you will have your photographer present to take pictures," the organizer quipped.

What photographer?

So off I went to find a photographer.

One of the major topics planned for Bush's speech was social security reform. He planned to modernize the social security system by allowing younger workers to voluntarily invest a portion of their payroll taxes in the stock market. His plan was endorsed by Elliot "Tony" Roosevelt, the grandson of President Franklin Delano Roosevelt, considered the driving force behind establishing the social security system. To support this theme, Thermagon was asked to select four employees that met certain specified profiles. For example, one was a single mother. The Bush team then applied their social security reform plans to each selected employee's individual situation to demonstrate the advantages of his plan. When Governor George W. Bush arrived, they each had personal interviews with him. These selected employees were seated on stools behind Governor Bush as he spoke.

By Thursday, the Bush team had installed their own independent phone system in case of an emergency. Bomb sniffing German Sheppard dogs were brought through, and machine guns were visible on the roof. Production at Thermagon managed to maintain some level of efficiency through Wednesday, but by Thursday, most all production efforts were lost. As part of the publicity, reporters from all over the world arrived to cover this event. The Latham family had assembled—my sons, of course, but also my mother, daughter, and one grandchild. My nerves were frayed, pacing the floor, awaiting the arrival of Governor George W. Bush. The Bush team told me that I was the hostess and was to be by Bush's side at all times and to not let the secret service get in my way. As Bush arrived through the back door onto our new hardwood floors, he walked toward me as if he were skating. He immediately put me at ease, and I quickly learned that he was very easy to communicate with. Accompanying him were Tony Roosevelt and Ohio Governor Robert Taft. The next two to three hours were spent with George W., touring the factory, overseeing the individual interviews of our employees and participating in the introductions preceding Bush's speech. After the speech, Bush mingled with the audience and answered questions. Besides social security, Bush spoke about his position on the strategic oil reserve. Vice President Al Gore, who was opposing Bush for president, favored tapping into the oil reserve as a means to manipulate oil prices. Bush, on the other hand, was against tapping into the oil reserve, believing that would be a national security risk. The visit was capped off with personal discussions with myself and my sons. During the course of the visit, one of my employees asked, "If you become president, will you come back?"

To which he answered "yes."

In the aftermath of this visit, many people, including political types, business associates, and friends asked me how I was able to persuade the Bush campaign to send him to Thermagon. Few believed me when I revealed that I had never in my life made financial contributions to a political candidate.

I swear that to be true.

Not long after the Bush visit, I was invited to Governor Taft's home in Columbus for dinner. While there, I was asked by several people how I was able to engineer a visit from George W. Bush. My answer, "If you don't know, how do you expect me to know?"

Soon after this visit, I had a phone call from Mike Hofman, the reporter who had written articles about me in *Inc. Magazine.* He asked if he could be present with me at an election evening event in Cleveland to watch the election results as they came in. I was not overly anxious to organize this, but I complied. I found a space, rented a television, contracted a caterer, invited a few guests, and hosted the event. Mike said that one other company on the *Inc. 500* had received a visit from Al Gore and that an *Inc.* reporter was, likewise, going to visit them for an election evening event.

You may remember the 2000 election and the bitter battle for the White House. Early in the evening, it looked like Gore was a winner. Florida was expected to be the deciding state and television networks started awarding the twenty-five electoral votes from Florida to Al Gore, even before the polls were closed in the Florida

Panhandle. Less than two hours later, Voter News Service (VNS) issued a bulletin stating, "We're canceling the vote in County 16," a reference to Duval County, which includes Jacksonville. VNS realized they'd gotten inaccurate returns from traditionally Republican precincts in Duval. By 10:00 p.m., networks began rescinding projections of Florida for Gore.

As Ohio, Tennessee, and Arkansas fell to Bush, the race for electoral and popular votes settled into a virtual tie. With a shrug of the shoulders, my guests all agreed that it was time to go home and sleep on the events of this anticlimactic evening.

For the next thirty-six days, Bush and Gore, multitudes of attorneys, the Florida Supreme Court, and the US Supreme Court all battled back and forth on how to determine the outcome of the election. After hanging chads, not-so-hanging chads, misinterpreted instructions, recounts and hand counts, and deadlines to meet, the courts finally decided that it was too late for Florida to correct the many discrepancies in their voting process, and the winner was declared George W. Bush.

In reflection on how this visit came to be, I began realizing that maybe the abundance of publicity from the likes of *Inc. Magazine* gave political candidates the notion to court female CEOs of fast-growing companies. When candidates link themselves to successful women entrepreneurs, other women voters may respond. The battle for the women's vote had certainly heated up. So rather than cajoling candidates to visit their company, female entrepreneurs discovered that campaigners sought them out so that they could be seen at these successful businesses. Hanging out with successful female CEOs for electoral success became rated right up there with kissing babies.

THE TURN OF
THE CENTURY

CHAPTER TWENTY-THREE

THE DOT-COM BUST

Nothing ever goes straight up.

Thermagon's tremendous success and growth through the year 2000 can be attributed, at least in part, to the same factors that drove the dot-com bubble, occurring roughly from 1997 to 2001. The historic economic bubble was a period of excessive speculation and extreme growth in the usage and adaption of the internet by businesses and consumers. During this period, many internet-based companies were commonly referred to as "dot-coms." This commercial growth of the internet was sparked by the advent of the World Wide Web and then the release of the Mosaic web browser. In the late nineties, the reduction of the "digital divide," advances in internet connectivity, increases in uses for the internet, and greater education on the use of the internet led to further increases of internet usage. The "digital divide" is the gap between those who have ready access to computers and the internet and those who do not. The percentage of households in the United States owning computers grew from 15 percent to 35 percent between 1990 and 1997. This shift to an economy based on computerization is known as the Information Age.

As a result of the rapidly increasing usage of the internet, many investors were eager to invest, at any valuation, in any company that had one of the internet-related prefixes or a ".com" suffix in its name, leading to a stock market bubble. During the bubble, the valuations of companies increased rapidly. A combination of rapidly rising stock prices, market confidence that the companies would turn future profits, speculation in stocks by individuals and widely available venture capital created an environment where many investors overlooked traditional metrics, such as price-earnings ratio, in favor of basing confidence on technological advancements.

An unprecedented amount of personal investing occurred during the boom and the press reported the phenomenon of people quitting their jobs to engage in full-time day trading. For example, the craftsman, furniture designer, and cabinet maker, who resided in our building, spent much of his time trading in the market rather than building furniture. At the height of the boom, it was possible for a promising dot-com company to become a public company via an initial public offering (IPO) and raise a substantial amount of money even though it had never made a profit or, in some cases, realized any revenue whatsoever. News media such as *Forbes* and *The Wall Street Journal*, as well as Federal Reserve Chairman Alan Greenspan were known to encourage the public's desire to invest in these unprofitable dot-com companies.

The value of the Nasdaq composite stock market index, which includes many technology companies, rose from one thousand in 1995 to five thousand in the year 2000. By the end of the nineties, the Nasdaq reached a price-earnings ratio of two hundred. In 1999, Qualcomm rose in value by 2,619 percent and twelve other large-cap stocks each rose over 1,000 percent. Cisco Systems, a provider of router and switch hardware for network systems was founded in 1984 and had an IPO in 1990 with its stock price increasing 24 percent the first day. By 2000, Cisco reached a stock price of $79 and a market cap of $546B, greater than Microsoft and considered the most valuable company in the world. By 2001, its stock fell to $10 and its market cap to nearly $100B. They had been ramping up production and expectations to unreasonable levels during the late nineties.

During this time Thermagon had been working with Qualcomm and had acquired Cisco systems as a major customer for our insulated metal circuit boards. In the first quarter of 2001, over $1 million worth of Cisco business just went away, seemingly overnight.

Contract manufacturers for the computer industry started canceling orders. As a result of this dot-com bust, Thermagon's revenue fell more than $2 million in the first quarter over fourth-quarter revenue in 2000.

Granted, quarter over quarter, sales increases cannot be expected to go on forever, but such a sudden and steep decline was difficult for Thermagon to imagine.

Let's take a moment and pause to think about what has just happened. Technology had just been attacked by its own innovation. Technology sales had just shrunk for the first time in two decades. The biggest companies in Silicon Valley had just lost $90 billion, more than their profit for the past eight years. Computer and communications systems were used to monitor customer demand and manage the production of goods and services. Missed forecasts and massive overproduction marked the electronic recession. Technology had just outpaced human capabilities. People do not get cheaper, faster, and better every eighteen months, as described in Moore's law for electronics. Human ability simply could not understand what was going on and did not have the capacity to keep up with the data being generated. Industry overproduced its market demand. Companies, more than ever, now needed to differentiate their products and services so that price would not become the basis for competition.

Luckily, Thermagon maintained a conservative approach to business. The company had little to no debt was watching bookings closely to detect any softness in the market and continued to work closely with customers to understand what was needed in new product development. However, we had geared up staff and manufacturing capability in anticipation of future growth. How we managed the downturn while still maintaining profitability, as well as the morale of the company, is a unique story.

Initially, we believed that the downturn would be short-lived and that the strength of the market would return just as quickly as it vanished. Thermagon began to delay equipment additions and let go of temporary production personnel. We realized that we had excess production staff on hand, but we were reluctant to reduce staff because of the difficulties in bringing them back when sales would pick up again, not to mention the effect on each of their families. Instead, we enlisted everyone in every department to provide ideas to help us manage our money better. We called this program the "War on Waste." Through our employee's suggestions, we scored successes ranging from smarter ways to purchase needed items to more efficient ways to sustain the facility, to process changes that increased the yield in our products, and to reduced scrap rates. Lots of employees pitched in and money was saved!

You might remember that each month, Thermagon had an all company meeting to discuss the status of the business and any current issues. The employees knew we were overstaffed for they were not busy. We explained in the meetings that we were trying very hard to maintain everyone's job. We encouraged employees to participate in our on-site classes. We offered time off without pay with the promise that their job was not in jeopardy. Our sincerity was real, and the employees knew it. By the middle of the second quarter, it became apparent that stronger measures were needed to keep the company profitable. We reduced advertising, travel, outside consultant services, and payroll costs. Each salaried employee gave up 10 percent of their earnings for the second half of 2001. We called another all-employee meeting and explained what we were doing and laid out the probability that we would need to reduce staff.

My experience with BP and with colleagues taught me that letting go several employees each week over a period of time was a very debilitating process. It creates the passing of rumors, the fear of who will be next to leave and causes instability, poor morale, and loss of productivity. Even so, this was often the process for downsizing in many corporations. That would not be the process used by Thermagon. Many hours went into planning our next move. Our general manager managed the plan with very close help from my youngest son Craig. They dealt with questions such as the following: How many employees needed to go? What departments should be affected? What process would we use? How long would it take to complete? The answers were as follows: thirty employees or approximately one-third of our workforce would be leaving, all departments of Thermagon would be affected, four of our managers would participate simultaneously in conducting the exit interviews, and the process would take no more than half of a workday.

We were thoughtful and did our best to be fair in our selections. We did all this with the view of reshaping the organization to position ourselves correctly for the expected return of our markets. As you can imagine, this was a difficult process. On the day of the layoff, all employees slated to leave were notified, interviewed, and had exited the building by noon. At that time, I called another all-company meeting. At this meeting, we took time to literally mourn the loss of those people who were our friends over the past months and who would no longer be with us. I, as well as the employees, had the opportunity to express our sadness for what had just happened. I then rallied the remainder of our workforce and reminded them that they were the chosen ones and that together we would lead Thermagon to future success.

As we moved forward without the hectic pace of the year 2000, our attention was focused on how best to deal with the economic slowdown of 2001 and 2002. If the dot-com bust did not make the outlook glum enough, the events of 9/11/2001 only made them worse. The Islamic attacks caused a setback for every aspect of business. Realizing that America was under attack, the stock market did not open on 9/11 and stayed closed until 9/17. When it reopened, the Dow Jones (DJ) went down 684 points or 7.1 percent, the most significant decline ever for one day. By Friday of that week, the DJ was down 1,370 points or 14 percent, a loss of $1.4T for the week. Hardest hit were the airlines, followed by tourism, hospitality, entertainment, and financial services. Consumer confidence also dropped to a very low level. Other industries benefited, such as defense-related business.

If all that bad news in one year was not enough, the Enron scandal became public in October 2001 and eventually led to its bankruptcy and the de facto dissolution of Arthur Andersen. Enron Corporation, an American energy company, based in Houston, Texas, was able to hide billions of dollars of debt from failed deals and projects by the use of accounting loopholes, special purpose entities, and poor financial reporting.

Arthur Andersen, Enron's auditors and one of the five largest audit and accountancy partnerships in the world, was pressured by Enron's board of directors and audit committee to ignore the issues. Enron filed for bankruptcy in December 2001. Arthur Andersen was found guilty of illegally destroying documents relevant to the Security and Exchange Commission (SEC) investigation that voided its license to audit public companies, effectively closing the business. These events truly shook the business community and led to the Sarbanes-Oxley Act. This act created layers of scrutiny for all companies and takes many costly hours to implement. For Thermagon, these events were not just one more hurdle for businesses to overcome but also created drama for my mentor and partner of Arthur Anderson, Paul. We agonized through those months with him. As is often the case, a few mistakes by a few people were enough to create the fall of one of the largest and most reputable accounting firms in the world.

Once we experienced the sudden drop in sales revenue in the first quarter of 2001, sales revenue remained relatively flat through the end of the first quarter of 2003, in the $2–3 million range per quarter. Sales were projected to be $14 million for the year 2002, a strong rebound from the $11 million in sales revenue of 2001. That was not to be. The effects of computing and the Information Age were beginning to settle in. The world of electronics appeared to be taking a pause, a deep breath if you will, and absorbing what had been taking place over the past ten years. Revolutionary innovation had slowed. Gadgets like phones with cameras, iPods, iTunes music store, radio-controlled automation, and Segways slowly began to appear. Computers continued to become faster and more comprehensive with graphics and video cards. Thermagon's business in computing remained steady but was not growing. Telecommunications and networking systems declined dramatically. As a result, our yearly sales for 2002 were only $10.5 million with $1 million net profit. We had no reason to believe that we were losing market share, but the overall market was down. Our revenue was down 7 percent in 2002 as compared to 20 to 25 percent for our competitors.

How Thermagon remained strong and viable through these difficult years is a testament to their tenacity, yet attentive management style. We held the line on unneeded spending and kept the company profitable. We invested in those things that we believed would increase the future value of the company, such as our sales and marketing efforts, new products, our quality systems, and a strategic plan.

Jim had assumed the leadership in sales and marketing in 2001. He grew the department by adding a sales manager and three regional sales engineers, plus one customer service person. We launched our website. Jim led our emphasis going forward to promote our Gap Fillers where we had several new products. He planned to pursue new markets in Europe and Asia. He had high expectations that the notebook computer business would improve. Much of the design-in of our materials remained in the United States while an increasing amount of manufacturing moved to Asia. This meant building strong relationships across both continents.

The Thermagon research and development department operated in lockstep with marketing, listening and responding to the needs of our customers. New products were being developed, and old ones were being improved. A new revolutionary phase-change material was developed using low-melting alloys. The theory was to place the low-melting alloy pad under the device to be cooled at room temperature while it was in solid form. As the device was turned on, it would heat up, and the low-melting alloy would melt and form a liquid, thus filling nearly perfectly the space and imperfections between the device and the heat spreader. Thermally, this performed magnificently. Since the material was made from metal alloys, it was electrically conductive, as well as thermally conductive. Therefore, care needed to be taken to assure that the liquid metal did not escape the interface and run onto the surrounding circuitry and electrically short the circuit. Various techniques were devised to prevent these potential electrical failures. My team was granted several patents on this technology.

Several products were modified to receive the Underwriters Laboratory's VO rating for flame retardancy. Our circuit board pre-

preg (adhesive film) was made thinner to four thousandths of an inch successfully to achieve Underwriters Laboratory (UL) approval for dielectric strength.

Our new gap-filler materials needed to be scaled up in production in order to meet the expected demand cost-effectively. Process changes were required, and new equipment had to be added. New machines were developed in conjunction with operations to manufacture our low melting alloy product, as well as other polymer-based phase-change materials. Sophisticated thermal resistance testing apparatus was also developed. All were contributing to the future value of the company.

One of the significant accomplishments of this era was the development of our quality systems. Our ultimate goal was to achieve ISO 9001 qualification. ISO, International Organization for Standardization, is a worldwide federation of quality professionals who generate specific standards for excellence in business systems. It is based on seven quality management principles: strong customer focus, leadership, engagement of people, a process approach, continued improvement, evidence-based decision-making, and relationship management. Achieving formal ISO qualification means adherence to best practices across an organization. It is a long process that can take years. It is an accomplishment that provides a company with instant worldwide credibility about the quality of the design, manufacturing, and service of its products. The team at Thermagon invested hundreds of hours perfecting our business processes and documenting our procedures, instructions, and results. With each day's efforts, we were making our company more productive and professional. Our goal was to become fully compliant and be accredited by an ISO auditor by late 2002. That meant that close to four hundred documents were written, reviewed, approved, and published. All these documents then needed to be formally audited. We trained eight internal people, working in teams, conducted forty-one separate internal audits to confirm that all our business processes were working as designed. When issues or imperfections were found in any of these processes, we logged the problem, assessed its importance, and, if necessary, assigned formal corrective actions to be taken. Each corrective action was designed to improve the quality of what we produced and the service we provided, as well as save us money. This is called continuous improvement, and Thermagon was committed to it. The work involved every person in the company. By 2003, we were formally audited by an internationally accredited ISO registrar and became certified as an ISO 9001/2000 company. This told the world what our customers had always known that when you purchase from Thermagon, you are buying some of the best products in the world.

Another way, Thermagon attempted to strengthen their business processes and secure new markets as they progressed into a more favorable economic environment was to develop a strategic plan. I searched and found several facilitators who could help us with this process. I introduced them to the management team and let them choose which one they would prefer to work with.

The facilitator interviewed the management team one on one and spoke with many of the employees. The process was a collaborative procedure where all managers were expected to participate.

The outline of our plan was as follows:

Core Purpose is to take technology to market in a way that provides the best value for customers.

Core values:

- ➢ Care about employees
- ➢ Motivated to get results
- ➢ Innovation and creativity are encouraged
- ➢ Honesty and integrity are valued
- ➢ React quickly and flexibly to customer needs

Company vision:

- ➢ Solidify our position as the leading innovator and manufacturer of the highest performance thermal management materials.
- ➢ Materials will serve existing and new market needs worldwide

> By 2005, achieve revenues of $25 million with profit at 20 percent of revenue
> No plans to sell the business

The seven strategic areas addressed in the plan for 2003–2005:

> Stronger customer relationships
> Commercialize our seven new products into new markets such as memory, logic, LED lighting, audio equipment, military, and video cards
> Get products to market faster
> Develop next-generation products
> Support existing profitable products
> Access all products regularly
> Implement continuous improvement

Details of the strategic plan provided objectives for twelve to eighteen months with assigned tasks and metrics to evaluate the progress of implementing the plan.

Even though these years were challenging for Thermagon, many positive outcomes can be noted. We learned how to downsize the company without destroying its morale. All remaining employees stayed with us for many years. We learned that revenue growth does not go up indefinitely. We learned that we could successfully manage our way through a significant downturn. Thermagon remained profitable throughout both years. We improved the company by attaining our ISO designation, (emphasizing and) growing the sales and marketing team, continuing to create new products, and developing a strategic plan.

CHAPTER TWENTY-FOUR

PAUSE TO EVALUATE

*Being a good businessperson does not make you
an entrepreneur.*

Thermagon has become an established company, recognized as a major player in the thermal management of electronics throughout the world from North America to Europe to Asia. The company has managed its way through two declining sales years while maintaining profits in both years. We entered the year 2003 with much optimism for future growth.

Now that the company is established with a complete management team and a strategic plan for the next several years, my role as the CEO has changed dramatically. Having spent the past twelve years creating a company based on proprietary technology, I, along with my family and team, was able through considerable hands-on efforts to accomplish the following:

- ➢ Raise adequate funds from angel investors to launch and maintain the business
- ➢ Create a technology for providing much-needed high thermally conductive materials for the electronics industry
- ➢ Develop a process for manufacturing the materials cost-effectively
- ➢ Attain and develop a dedicated workforce
- ➢ Secure a talented management team

> ➤ Provide a state-of-the-art manufacturing facility with room for expansion
> ➤ Acquire ISO 9001 certification

To accomplish these successes required significant multidisciplinary skills and hands-on work in the day-to-day operations of the company. My role moving forward looks quite different. I believe that it is vitally important for a developing CEO to recognize the importance of changing one's role in the company as the company matures. For example, managing a zero to $20 million company requires different skills than growing an established business into a $50-million company. Often inventors, founders and CEOs have difficulty making the needed changes as the company grows and often don't recognize the need for such a transition. For me, I now realized that I needed to reinvent myself.

The Thermagon management team was ready and fully capable of carrying out the day-to-day operations of the company. My job became one of leading and coaching so that the various departments of the company were working together toward mutually agreed goals. I set up a schedule to meet one on one with each of the managers monthly to implement this plan. In these meetings, I was always full of questions and curiosity about their work and progress. I needed to be the visionary of the company and continue to educate myself on emerging technologies so that our materials continued to meet the requirements for the thermal management needs of the future. I needed to promote the development of new materials to ensure our position as the leader in thermal performance. I needed to oversee investments for the future growth of the company. For example, issues like whether to continue manufacturing in our current location or move some portion of the manufacturing to China became a significant concern.

I intended to create a collaborative style of management as opposed to the historically more common type of command and control management like that of General Electric's Jack Welsh. The need for me to become an effective leader and a visionary weighed heavily on my mind. Questions like the following were rattling around in my head:

- ➢ How effective would I be in leading the team?
- ➢ Do I have all the right people on the bus, as Jim Collins references in his book *Good to Great*, stating the importance of hiring the right people for each corporate function?
- ➢ Have I found my true calling?
- ➢ Knowing full well that all products and technologies have a certain lifespan, whereby innovation reaches a plateau and further improvement becomes difficult, would I be able to continue to lead the change needed to provide the best thermal solutions for tomorrow's products?
- ➢ Can Thermagon continue to deliver their products or services cost-effectively and in a manner that gives it a real competitive advantage?

Prompted by this self-introspection and the advice of my strategic planning consultant, I decided to seek training that could improve my leadership and management skills. This consultant recommended a coaching program offered by the Gestalt Institute of Cleveland. An in-depth discussion on the theory supporting the Gestalt Coaching Program can be found in "The Journal of the Organization Development Network," volume 36, number 4, 2004. This program was not a weekend workshop, but instead, an in-depth training program offered in four one-week increments over six to nine months. Participating in such a program as a scientist turned CEO, along with other professionals experienced in the world of psychology and the arts, took me out of my comfort zone.

I began to realize that in this increasingly complex and chaotic world, interpersonal relationships had become increasingly important and more complicated. Through my experience at the Gestalt Institute, I began to learn that relating effectively with others can advance one's leadership and professional effectiveness, as well as one's personal relationships. Connecting well with others is based upon using our capacities to be self-aware, curious, and open to another's experience and viewpoint, as well as having the skills to communicate effectively to influence with integrity.

The Gestalt system believes that the true worth of coaches is not measured by the set of skills or tools they possess but by their ability to see themselves clearly in relation to others. Such clarity drives the individual to integrate system change, producing powerful interventions with outstanding results. I learned that change and resistance are inseparable and two sides of the same thing. I learned the difference between a problem and a dilemma. A problem has a solution. A dilemma is the presence of inherently conflicting forces in a system. The forces are natural, predictable, and unavoidable. Dilemmas cannot be solved, only managed. For example, should employees be learning in their job or performing? The answer is yes to both, and therefore, a dilemma that needs to be managed.

As I launched my plans for self-improvement, other events were coinciding. I was pleased with my decision to participate in the program at the Gestalt Institute. However, I continued to be restless. I was feeling a bit out of sorts and unmotivated. My sense of urgency had gone or maybe was no longer needed. Life at Thermagon had transitioned to something entirely different from what I remembered from just a few years before. Business was going well with all primary indicators pointing in a positive direction. All I needed to do was to keep the team motivated and create a vision for the future.

Shouldn't that be enough?

CHAPTER TWENTY-FIVE

MY DILEMMA

Hard decisions come with owning your own business.

I t is true that I had entered my last trimester of life at age sixty-two. I still had plenty of energy. I was depending on my "rolling" five-year business projections for validation of continued business success. A rolling five-year plan is one that considers the current year, plus the following four years. Therefore, each year you are evaluating existing projections and adding an additional year. You can see that in 2003, I was projecting out to 2008, when I would be sixty-eight years old. How frightening was that? Maybe this rolling five-year plan wasn't such a good idea. The concept came from one of the speakers from TEC, my group of CEOs who often acted as my advisory board.

Not only was my age bothering me, I recalled an astute businessman, Harry S. Dent, as I mentioned earlier, who believed that significant economic change would occur around 2008. Could his projections have credence? When would be the right time to cash out of Thermagon? How long would my investors want to wait to recoup their investment plus the projected gains? For me, I realized that all my assets were in one place invested in Thermagon.

Was It Wise to Have All My Eggs in One Basket?

Family businesses are never easy to maintain. Family members are always managing dual roles. For my sons and me, we were living the roles of mother and sons, as well as roles of CEO and managers. Very different behaviors are appropriate for each role. It appeared to me, at least on the surface, that minimal conflict was generated as a result of the workings of the family members. Nevertheless, the emotional impact from the existing family members on the current employees and future employees was tough to evaluate. The situation seemed acceptable and manageable, if not ideal.

As you may recall, companies called Thermagon on a regular basis to discuss the possibility of an acquisition. The discussions all ended on the same note.

"The company is not for sale!"

My sons were included in the discussions, whenever possible, and often had varying opinions on the possibility of considering a sale of Thermagon. Their parting words were always, "It's your decision, Mom."

From an intellectual perspective, it appeared evident that myself and the investors had an interest in cashing out some part of their investment in Thermagon. A multitude of deals was possible from a financial buyer purchasing a portion of Thermagon to a strategic buyer buying the whole company, as well as any combination in between. From needing to reinvent myself to a need to cash out on some portion of my life's dream and successes, I was now faced with decisions of monumental proportions.

The decisions that I found myself faced with were genuinely gut-wrenching. Thermagon was my baby. I created it through significant sacrifice and risk of legal issues and financial disaster. Emotionally, how could I even think of letting even a portion of it go? I created a company culture that put an unprecedented value on each employee. How could I betray them? If I were to sell the company, would my legacy be destroyed? Would I miss the prestige and status of being the CEO of a successful company? Would my manufacturer's representatives suffer hardship if I were to sell Thermagon to a company who insisted on taking all sales direct? Would I miss my relationships with colleagues all over the world?

The answer to these conflicting circumstances and decisions had no right or wrong solutions. The answer was about choices, making a choice that had the least detrimental effect to all involved. For me, I think the overriding factor that I loved most was the experience of creating a company and the excitement and sense of urgency needed to be successful. That, in and of itself, motivated me more than pursuing the task of taking an existing company to the next level of excellence. As I soul searched the answers to the questions before me, I began to realize that I had accomplished my goal of taking a technology to market and creating a company that succeeded in ways that I had not even imagined. Thermagon's technology had promoted the advancement of computing in the Information Age by allowing systems to perform without the limitations of heat.

Is That the Definition of a Real Entrepreneur?

Formulating monumental decisions that change the course of a company and that significantly change lives needs to be studied and critiqued carefully overtime. I chose to call it a process. Concerns on how I would cash out did not weigh heavily on my mind in the early years of Thermagon. It was not until 1995 and the purchase offer from Chomerics that I gave much thought to the possibility of how to cash out, either for myself or my investors.

As the inquiries and interest from companies wanting to purchase Thermagon continued, it became impossible to ignore the thought of how the company, my "baby," would move forward without me when I decided to retire or move on. This thought process began with the intent to grow the company to at least $10 to $20 million dollars in revenue and become the leading supplier of thermal materials for electronics. This continued growth would command further interest in potential buyers and generate publicity worldwide. Once these goals were attained, I could look more sensibly toward my next steps. The good news was that I had many options. Besides continuing as we currently existed, I perceived two other potential paths to follow.

The first path would be to step down as CEO and promote one of my sons to the position. That, however, would raise the apparent issues of jealousy within the family and could be controversial with other managers and employees. Neither son had experience in growing or managing a company, but both had an in-depth understanding of the business. I could promote a nonfamily manager to CEO, but no one stood out as a likely candidate. It would also be possible to hire a highly trained, skilled, and experienced person from outside the company as CEO. I spent many hours noodling on these choices. Could I be satisfied or happy just turning the company along with all my assets over to someone else to manage? My conclusion was that no matter how skilled, honest, or attached the proposed person turned out to be, I could not just walk away and let someone else take over. It would have been like a mother leaving her child before his or her time.

The second path would be to sell all or part of the company. Purchasers of companies are generally divided into two categories. First, there is the financial buyer. This type of buyer is interested mainly in the financial return on his investment. Increasing cash flow is essential. Therefore, this buyer will be anxious to increase revenue and cut costs. Often a financial buyer's deal is very leveraged, such that his lenders become like partners. He is most likely to keep on the existing management. A financial buyer may consider buying only a portion of a company. However, he would be unlikely to buy out the founder or management team and more likely to buy out the investors. This choice was not likely to meet my needs for wanting to cash out and was generally going to only pay the intrinsic value of the company or the portion thereof.

Second is the strategic buyer, someone who acquires a company with similar or synergistic aspects, so that the resulting whole becomes greater than the sum of its parts. They are looking for long-term value creation and are interested in cost cutting often by eliminating overlapping departments or functions. The synergies can provide an opportunity for increasing revenue and enhancing productivity. Consequently, strategic buyers usually will pay a premium for a company with the hopes of creating value that is greater than the sum of its parts. Of the many companies who expressed an interest in acquiring Thermagon, all could be considered strategic buyers.

Like most difficult decisions, no choice will satisfy all concerns. The pros and cons of each option need to be thought out carefully and weighed against the status quo. An argument can be made for keeping the status quo or managing the business while maintaining the current structure. I could continue to improve my skills and reinvent myself. Sales could likely grow moderately, even without the synergistic effect of a strategic buyer. The corporate culture could be maintained with employee loyalty remaining high. I could enjoy the prestige and status that comes with being the CEO of a successful company. I could hopefully find satisfaction in maintaining the success of the company. I could revel in the thought that Thermagon would carry on through the ages from one family member to another and thus create my legacy. This all is assuming that no one neglects the business along the way nor makes devastating decisions that would drive the company into bankruptcy.

How Fortunate Was I to Have Had So Many Choices!

I believed that whatever decision I made at that point, my sons would come out winners. From my perspective, being freed from their roles at Thermagon would allow them to pursue their ideas and dreams with far more resources than I, or most other people, would have access to. Together, Jim and Craig owned one-third of Thermagon. As with me, Jim and Craig's assets were primarily invested in Thermagon. Continuing in their roles or similar managerial roles at Thermagon for the foreseeable future could have provided them with a sense of security.

Jim and Craig's personalities are different, and I chose not to speculate on their preferred route, but I can only imagine that either scenario could have been perceived as a winning situation.

Over the course of ten years, I had drawn an imaginary line in the sand over that I must not step unless, one day, I determined that I was willing to entertain a discussion about the possibility of a Thermagon acquisition. Once a decision was made to pursue an acquisition, standard procedure is to hire a firm to manage the process and negotiations. Such a firm would prepare a "book" on Thermagon, which would be a promotional story about Thermagon with financial data and projections. This book would be distributed to a list of prospective buyers, formally announcing the company's desire to be acquired. An auction, of sorts, would follow with offers from interested parties along with transaction details presented for company review. Presumably, the potential acquirer with the highest bid would be given a chance to participate in the due diligence process and negotiate a final agreement. Keep in mind that many deals fall through during this negotiation process.

Crazy as it may sound, the thought of going through this formal and public process of selling one's business was offensive to me. I wanted to choose the company with whom to negotiate, and I wanted it to be a secret so that my employees and the community would not become anxious. The due diligence process and negotiations toward a corporate acquisition only become a reality when the money arrives in your bank account. Then and only then was it time to make announcements to employees and the business community. In the event that I would have considered moving forward with an acquisition, that described the process that was most comfortable for me.

Having sat through dozens of meetings with prospective buyers, I was always careful not to step over the imaginary line I had drawn in the sand, which would tip my hand away from my position that the company was not for sale. By mid-2003, my hours of contemplation seemed to be leading me closer to a possible acquisition. I preferred midsize companies of less than $1 billion dollars in revenue and ones that truly had synergistic components that could enhance the value of Thermagon. Material-based companies that merely wanted to add thermal materials for the electronics industry to their existing offerings because it was a profitable, growing field generated less interest.

When one is contemplating selling their "baby," visualizing how the company would operate under new management became critical. The chances are that a purchaser would require me to stay employed with them for one to two years. Change from the existing status quo was inevitable. I would need to be prepared for such a change and be okay with it. Being physically present, yet not in charge and making the decisions would surely be very difficult. It was impossible to predict what changes would occur and at what rate, but one certainty was that change would happen. At best, I would need to savor the advisory capacity and restrain any judgment concerning their decisions. Realizing the probable scenario that would occur once the business was sold provided a somewhat realistic insight into what the experience might be like. No one likes too many surprises. I also contracted McDonald Investments to assist me in the process of evaluating potential buyers and to assist in any negotiations that may have ensued.

CHAPTER TWENTY-SIX

THE DEAL

Success comes from a strong sense of time and an understanding of the sequence of events occurring around you.

Having contemplated the many paths forward, I had narrowed my decision down to two options: pursuing an acquisition or proceeding with the status quo for the time being. I now believed that I must be a true entrepreneur, for taking the business to the next level of success did not motivate or excite me. As difficult as the decision can be to sell your baby, I was now, on my own terms, willing to proceed with the process of pursuing an acquisition of Thermagon. Over the course of a few months, representatives from one company found a reason to be in Cleveland several times and requested to meet for lunch or dinner with me. It became apparent that they were determined to be in the thermal material space, if not with Thermagon, with one of our competitors. There was a synergy in combining their existing EMI Shielding business with the thermal business. There were obvious customer overlaps and potential manufacturing synergies. This company was about $750 million in revenue, just small enough in size to allow Thermagon to make an impact, and yet large enough to have the resources to create synergy or added value to both companies.

In one of these meetings over lunch, I can remember vividly stepping over my imaginary line. The company was Laird Technologies. I began to ask the "what-if" questions that revealed my willingness to consider the possibility of an acquisition. Mark, my representative from McDonald Investments, was accompanying me and could guide me through this process. McDonald Investments does not receive remuneration based on hours worked but rather on a percentage of the final value of the acquisition. As one question led to another, I soon found myself being asked if I would consider signing a letter of intent.

A letter of intent states the interest of both parties, buyer and seller, to negotiate a final and binding agreement between the two companies. The letter spells out the details needed for confidentiality, defines the time allotted for either party to terminate the discussions or complete an acquisition, and lays the grounds for due diligence. The letter is considered nonbinding, except that the seller agrees to refrain from conversations with other potential buyers until the termination of intent or completion of an agreement is reached.

Besides Mark, no one else was involved in the decision to sign such a letter of intent, except for myself. I signed the letter and informed my sons immediately thereafter. They were somewhat surprised but very supportive of my decision. Remember, they always deferred when the subject was discussed to the statement, "It is your decision, Mom."

I intended to keep this process very secret and under the radar screen. I needed my management team to assist in the due diligence process, so I shared the decision with the management on the grounds of complete confidentiality and a piece of the final settlement. I was very concerned about losing the great morale of the company and did not want the remainder of the employees to learn about the possible sale. Laird, the potential buyer, was very aware of my need for confidentiality and respected my requirements to uphold these requests. For example, Laird agreed to tour our plant and facility at six o'clock in the morning before our employees arrived.

The process of due diligence is a comprehensive exercise to help the buyer understand what they are buying, what obligations they are assuming, what problematic liabilities or risks may exist, along with intellectual property issues. To keep the company operating smoothly and profitably during this process, I engaged outside help. Along with McDonald Investments, I contracted with Baker Hostetler LLP to be the lead negotiator of the sales process. They would manage the process of due diligence with help from McDonald Investments, myself, Paul, my close confidant and mentor, the Thermagon management team and our accountants.

The due diligence process is of utmost importance when the company being purchased is a private company, such as Thermagon. Private companies have not been subject to public scrutiny as would be the case for a public company. Very little information can be acquired from public sources, making the due diligence process of vital importance.

The financial data is generally, first and foremost, in the eyes of a purchaser, which can include historical financial statements, as well as projections. Also included are income statements, balance sheets, and cash flow analysis. These statements would reveal Thermagon's profitability and would be a positive driver to valuing the company. Since Thermagon held its intellectual property as a trade secret, understanding the proprietary nature of the technology would be of keen interest to Laird and a significant part of the due diligence process. The more recent patents would also be of interest.

Thermagon's customer base and sales channels were vitally important to Laird since they were crucial to their strategic fit with us. There was much overlap in their current business customers with Thermagon's, which would allow them to streamline their sales channels. This was one of several areas where Laird could add value. The contracts with our sales representatives worldwide were carefully reviewed. Our product literature, price lists and surveys were all examined as part of the due diligence. Also of interest were the advantages and disadvantages of Thermagon's products and their technology as compared to our competitors. Our material supply chain would be examined for availability and sourcing issues, as well as for any synergy with Laird's existing raw materials. Thermagon's supply agreement with St. Gobain was of particular interest.

Even though Thermagon's production process was 100 percent solids and environmentally friendly, Laird was extremely concerned about environmental issues with the land on which Thermagon resided. Had it been contaminated by some previous owner unbeknownst to us. Laird had a lousy experience when purchasing another company that resided on contaminated land that led to a lawsuit. As a result, Thermagon was held responsible for any contamination issues to the soil under and around our building for several years after the conclusion of the deal. That led Thermagon to reserve funds from the sale of the company in escrow until the danger of an environmental lawsuit had passed.

The production area of Thermagon's facility was of particular interest to Laird since it is a vital part of our intellectual property and trade secrets. The possibility of combining production space with their current process was another key to the strategic fit of the two companies. Their space and connections in China could be useful to future production of Thermagon products.

Thermagon's counsel, Baker Hostetler, managed our online data room. The online data room organized and made available all the dozens of documents required for review in the due diligence process. This was a detailed and very time-consuming process.

Concurrently, with this due diligence process, Baker Hostetler was negotiating the terms of a purchase agreement that would be acceptable to both parties. Laird was interested in purchasing the business and assets of Thermagon by way of a transaction for the entire issued stock. From the information received through due diligence, Laird was able to value the company based on a multiple of earnings before interest and taxes (EBIT). After much back and forth negotiations, a value was placed on Thermagon. Laird offered an initial cash payment of about two-thirds of the value in cash to be followed by earn-out payments in the following two years based on a formula using net revenue relative to projections. Earn-out payments are a way to maximize the sales price of the company based on one's belief that the revenue will continue to grow significantly over the next two years.

It is a monumental task to complete the work involved to bring an acquisition to a satisfactory and successful conclusion. For Thermagon; it involved McDonald Investments, Baker Hostetler, our accountants, the Thermagon management team, as well as myself. For Laird, a similar entourage of people was needed to complete this process. The time required for the process from the signing of the letter of intent to a completed deal was about one year. My investors were not informed until very late in the process. In contrast to the employees, they were ecstatic with the news of a Thermagon acquisition. Ten plus years after their initial investment, they were able to cash out with a profit of forty times their original investment.

As I had hoped, the proceedings were kept confidential. Neither my employees, the local community, nor the thermal management industry was aware of the acquisition until the announcement on April 23, 2004. I assembled the entire company and proceeded to make the announcement. That is one of the hardest things I have ever had to do. The news was taken with much surprise and shock. Even though I had completed my personal goal and believed that the strategic fit with Laird would open doors and allow Thermagon to grow faster than it would on its own, change creates anxiety and concerns for all involved. I had a lot of explaining to do to assure my employees that the transition would go well.

One million dollars of my portion of the proceeds of the sale were reserved and distributed to the employees. About half was reserved for the management team who played a significant role in keeping confidentiality and providing information toward the success of the sale. The remainder of the money was distributed to the other employees and divided much like we had done when we gave our annual bonuses. I distributed the money to each employee, personally, amid a sea of emotion from tears to gratefulness and thanks. For me, I was ready to move on with the hope of promoting future entrepreneurship. I had just turned back into just plain "Mom."

CHAPTER TWENTY-SEVEN

THE RETURN OF THE UNEXPECTED

It always pays off to keep your promises.

H e said he would come back. Once again, the mystery centered around the person who was on the other end of the phone. It was spring 2004, and I'm knee deep in negotiations with Laird. As I answered the phone, the person said, "This is Julie from the White House."

Oh boy! I thought. *What white house is she referring to?*

Reluctant to believe one more time, I became convinced that Julie was, indeed, calling from *the* White House in Washington, DC. She proceeded to inform me that President George W. Bush was planning to be in Cleveland the following week to speak at the Women's Entrepreneurship in the Twenty-First Century Forum at the Cleveland Convention Center.

"That's nice," I said. "But unfortunately, I will be in California next week for a business conference and meetings."

Their plans seemed vague and unsettled. No specific mention was made about President Bush coming to Thermagon. I pondered the possibility of the president wanting to use our entrepreneurial story as part of his speech. Another call came in from the White House, still trying to formulate their plans for President Bush's visit to Cleveland the following Wednesday. I reiterated my plans to be in California the following week. With that, Julie from the White

House asked if there was someone else at Thermagon they could contact next week if needed.

"Certainly! You can call my son Craig Latham," I said, giving them his phone number. In passing, I told Craig that I had given his name and phone number to the White House.

"Not to worry," I said. "I feel quite confident that Thermagon is not in their plans."

So off to Silicon Valley I went that Monday morning, wholly engaged in the business at hand. I forgot about the calls from the White House. When I was having dinner with my business colleagues on Monday, the phone rang. It was Craig speaking in a desperate tone of voice, telling me that Bush was coming to Thermagon on Wednesday morning and that I needed to come home.

Whoa! Easier said than done.

I had an important meeting on Tuesday morning with Laird executives. I told Craig I would try to get a flight back Tuesday afternoon. He was already inundated with secret service people and the Bush entourage. I managed a late morning flight out of San Jose to Cleveland. Barely made the plane for the flight attendants were waiting for me to take my seat so that they could close the door of the plane and take off. It was a close call.

There was a three-hour time difference between Cleveland and California, so that meant it was already midafternoon on Tuesday afternoon when I took off. The evening darkness had set in by the time I landed in Cleveland. As we taxied to the terminal, I managed to see the large black jet on the runway that had transported the president's limousine. What was about to happen now seemed like a reality.

I jumped in a taxi cab and went directly to Thermagon, where I would receive my marching orders from the secret service. Bush was just a presidential candidate when he arrived before; now that he was the president of the United States, security was much tighter. The secret service and the Bush team literally took over the facility. Bush was not giving a major speech from Thermagon as before. His speech was to be at the Cleveland Convention Center. His intent at Thermagon was to greet our employees and tour the manufacturing facility. Craig had managed the process of arranging the president's visit with the secret service flawlessly. Jim and other Thermagon personnel stayed back in San Jose to continue our business there. I invited the Laird executives to come back with me if they were interested in meeting the president. They were tempted but declined.

As I arose the next day, I realized that I would have the honor of escorting George W. Bush through the Thermagon facility one more time. He said that he would come back. But who would have believed? I was my usual fidgety self until Bush arrived and soon recalled that he had a special knack of putting people at ease.

As he toured the factory, he made a special effort to greet each employee along the way. Thermagon employed many Hispanic ladies with whom he would speak in Spanish. Anytime he spotted a camera, he would stop to allow the employee to have a picture with him.

On the tour, Bush stopped along the way to help our workers prepare one of our key products for the pressing and curing step. I must say, he followed instruction very well. What an experience for our workers!

As Bush was working his way toward the exit, one of the Thermagon employees wished him well in his upcoming reelection campaign. His response was very poignant. He said, "The outcome of the election was up to the American people to decide and whatever the outcome...Laura still loves me."

As Bush approached the exit, he turned to me and asked, "Are you going to this gig downtown?"

"Yes," I replied.

"Come on! Ride with me," he said.

I could not believe what I was hearing. I think my mouth was going up and down, but no words were coming out. He asked if I had ever been in an armored limousine before.

"No," I quickly responded.

Craig and my employees went crazy running around from window to window screaming, "She went in the limo with the president!"

It was an extraordinary experience—riding to the convention center alone with President George W. Bush, along with the secret service and a motorcycle brigade surrounding us. The short trip gave me time to express my gratitude as well as my desire to meet Laura, who had not accompanied him on either visit.

Bush explained to me how he tries to share the accouterments of the office of the presidency with as many people as possible. He talked about entertaining fraternity brothers at the White House as an example.

When we arrived underground at the convention center, the secret service's only concern was for escorting the president into the facility safely. I became irrelevant. Not knowing exactly how to handle the situation, I walked with Bush as he greeted several waiting Cleveland dignitaries along the way. The situation seemed awkward to me, so I stepped aside and disappeared into the crowd.

My heart was beating frantically, and I must admit, the content of his speech was a blur. As I listened to his speech, I began to realize what had just happened. I left Thermagon spontaneously without a coat, my purse, or my cell phone. I realized that the president and the secret service would not be returning me to Thermagon. It was a strange feeling indeed. Needless to say, there were people in attendance who I knew and recognized. I soon found someone who happily agreed to give me a ride back to Thermagon. That day, March 10, 2004, was a day to remember!

LIFE AFTER
THERMAGON

CHAPTER TWENTY-EIGHT

SUCCESS IS NOT A GIVEN

Beware of people with claims too good to be true.

As anticipated, Laird stipulated in their closing documents that I was required to remain employed with them for two years to help in the transition. I knew this would be a difficult time for me. Laird immediately sent in a new person to manage the Thermagon operations. He became my new boss. I imagined that he would take over my office and kick me out to some open space. Thank goodness that never happened. I made some grueling trips to Asia and Europe with the CEO of Laird Technologies, trying to help with the transition. I was tasked with hiring some new employees, specifically out of the thermal management space. This was challenging and fraught with concerns of intellectual property infringement. I was also asked to evaluate businesses in the thermal space that could be complementary to Thermagon with the potential for acquisition. I found this process very interesting and insightful.

I was interested in helping Laird make Thermagon the best that it could be. It was helpful for me during this time to have the understanding that Laird was sure to take our sales direct as opposed to using manufacturers' representatives and to move much of our manufacturing to Asia. These were the globalization efforts that would take this thermal business to the next level. I felt compelled to personally visit my manufacturer's representatives to inform them that their contracts would be terminated as a result of the Thermagon sale. This was very sad and painful for me to do. I had built relationships with these "reps" and tried hard to train and nurture them with the mutual goal of growing sales.

Throughout my life, I had acquired a fascination for the use of electricity over gas-powered engines. I was the only one in my neighborhood who used an electric lawn mower. During my days at Thermagon, our materials were designed into the charging system of one of the first electric cars, the EV1. The EV1 was developed by General Motors (GM) in response to a government mandate in California for 2 percent of new cars to be zero emissions. GM produced 1,117 EV1 cars between 1996 and 1999. Companies like Aerovironment and AC Propulsion worked alongside GM in designing this car. Both companies were customers of Thermagon. These connections served to intensify my fascination for electric cars.

The EV1 cars were made available through limited lease-only agreements in specified western cities in California and Arizona. Customer reaction to the EV1 was quite positive. However, the strong lobby and power of the oil and automotive industries prevailed and through litigation with the California Air Resources Board (CARB) managed to diminish the zero-emissions vehicle (ZEV) stipulations. GM believed that electric cars occupied an unprofitable niche in the automobile market. As a result, GM discontinued the EV1 program in 2002, and all cars on the road were repossessed. Forty cars were donated to museums and educational institutions, albeit with deactivated power trains to keep the cars from ever running again, and the remainder were crushed in car compactors and destroyed. Hence, the production of the documentary, "Who Killed the Electric Car?"

The conventional business view of the EV1 as a failure is inherently controversial. If one considers the car a technological showpiece, an electric car that actually could replace a gasoline powered vehicle, it was truly a success. Certainly, the weakest link in the entire EV1 system was the battery. When the expected breakthrough in battery technology did not take place as expected, GM used this as one of its excuses for killing the car.

This whole electric car scenario piqued my interest and influenced future decisions. I proceeded among my circles of friends to talk up the success of the EV1 and how it demonstrated that technology existed that could replace the gas-powered car and lead to making the United States independent from Middle East oil. I was always quick to acknowledge that further advances in battery technology would be needed for any continued success in electric car development. One day, as I was expounding on my soapbox on the merits of electric car technology, a gentleman piped up and told me he knew someone who was starting a company based on new battery technology.

"Would you like me to introduce you to her?" he asked.

One could only imagine that I would respond with a resounding "yes!"

That "yes" changed my course for the years ahead. Simultaneously, with battery technology innovation, particularly in lithium-ion cells was the founding of Tesla Motors by Martin Eberhard and Marc Tarpenning. Elon Musk, who is often thought to be the founder of Tesla early on, became the largest investor in Tesla. Eberhard and Tarpenning thought they had found the perfect investor for Musk had the engineering smarts and the shared goal of trying to end the United States addiction to oil. As the largest shareholder of Tesla, Musk became chairman of the company and would later wield his position of strength to take control.

With this as a backdrop, I made my reservation for Boston to meet Christina, the founder of "The Battery Company," the generic name I assigned for the purposes of this book. The Battery Company was a battery start-up based on lithium-ion technology. Remember, I have just experienced success in my first attempt at being an entrepreneur. I thought to myself, "If I can make a success of an idea, others should be able to be successful as well." My success came with my having neither a PhD or an MBA.

When I met Christina, she appeared as a tall blond with a broad smile and an engaging personality. I was immediately intrigued for she also had an MS and a PhD from Uppsala University in Sweden and a postdoctoral appointment at Massachusetts Institution of Technology (MIT). She studied inorganic chemistry and now was an expert in electrochemistry.

Wow! What a combination!

I soon learned that she was also trained in music and considered a profession as an opera singer and was leading a choral group in the Boston area. Sorting my way through all this, it was her personality, bordering on theatrical, that drew me in.

Understanding the technology advantage of The Battery Company was a challenge for me. According to Christina, she had developed a new battery technology that could provide an improvement in runtime retention of up to five times and an increase in capacity up to 30 percent. She claimed that this could be accomplished with new and smaller battery-pack configuration, safer design, controlled failure mode, and with cost saving to the original equipment manufacturer (OEM). *Wow! What an improvement,* I thought. Her fastest path to sales was in the laptop computer market, which I knew from my experience at Thermagon, was growing and in need of better battery technology. Since I realized that the electric cars were early in their development, I was okay with entering the laptop computer market, which I understood was a stepping stone to electric cars.

Christina and I connected and stayed closely in touch after our meeting. I was still employed at Thermagon/Laird and managing that relationship along with searching for an understanding of Christina and her battery technology. Her enthusiasm and knowledge of the technology drew me in. I became very interested in contributing to the success of The Battery Company. I began talking about this company with my friends. As Christina started down this path to start her own business, I was there beside her. We became friends, and I made visits to her home and acquired a caring relationship with her family. As the months progressed, and the expenses accumulated, she became concerned about meeting her payroll. In I stepped to the rescue. I offered to raise seed money for The Battery Company to keep it afloat. Christina came to Cleveland several times to make presentations on the company's merits. My friends and business associates were the audiences. The year before, I had successfully sold my company and was a poster child for promoting young businesses. Because of my reputation, the interest escalated. In a short time, I had raised $1.8 million. This paid the bills until Christina wooed two venture firms, Gabriel Venture Partners and Venrock Partners to invest in The Battery Company. Gabriel Venture Partners is a California venture company providing seed capital for what they consider disruptive technology. They have an impressive track record. Venrock Partners, on the other hand, is an old-line venture firm that is known for its tagline, "Grow. Disrupt." Its early investments in Apple, Intel, Gilead Science, and the like have given them prestige in the business of venture capital. The investment and backing from these well-established venture firms allowed The Battery Company to launch the business, thanks to Carol Latham and her business associates for providing the lifeline months before. Christina and her engaging and masterful sales skills played a large role in making this happen. Few entrepreneurs, particularly females, are successful in convincing such prestigious venture firms to invest.

Quite a coup!

By the end of 2005, the company had made me chairman of the board, and I believed that the probability for success was high. My tenure at Laird/Thermagon was about to end in April 2006. In January of 2006, I asked Laird if I could break my contract and leave. They agreed that it was time for us to part ways, and I officially left Thermagon for what I thought was a great new adventure.

After my many trips to Boston, I decided to rent an apartment in the Gloucester building, located in the Back Bay section of Boston. In my attempts to make this habitable, there is a funny story I would like to share. I first had a bed delivered to this seventeenth-story apartment from Design Within Reach (DWR). When I returned home late one evening, I had no furniture except this bed that I had ordered. The bed frame was simple and easy to assemble. The mattress arrived in a small cylindrical package. Tired and with no other furniture in the place, I proceeded to put this bed together to have someplace to sleep. I began to remove the plastic surrounding the mattress. The bedroom was quite small, and this was, of course, a king-size bed.

Why? I am not sure.

As the plastic unraveled from the mattress, the mattress began to expand. Remember, this was in 2006, before foam mattresses were a popular item. As fate would have it, I was on the outside wall of the room as I began this process, seventeen floors above the ground. The door out of the room was on the opposite side of the room from me, and as I looked down behind me, I could see the ground seventeen floors below. The mattress became so large and heavy that I became trapped on the outside of the room away from the door.

Oh my!

Mind you, I was exhausted from a long day with nowhere to sleep except on this mattress. I was trapped with little strength left to weld this mattress in a position that would free me to reach the other side of the room. Think of Lucille Ball in the funny sitcom, *I Love Lucy*, and that was me struggling to make my way to freedom from this mattress. I was alone in Boston and not finding this so funny at the time, but as I reflect on the situation, it becomes increasingly humorous. I ultimately managed to conquer the problem and fell into bed for a few hours of sleep before I would make my way to The Battery Company offices in the morning.

Traveling in Boston by car was a unique challenge. Back Bay in Boston was plagued with one-way streets, and the freeway entrances took off in unexpected places with little markings. Boston drivers are well-known for their impatience and lack of attention to the rules of the road. As humorous as it sounds, it was quite an adventure. After my very first trip to Boston, I immediately purchased a portable GPS.

Life at The Battery Company was interesting and exciting. The laptop computer business was growing and had a tremendous need for lithium-ion batteries, particularly ones that could outperform the existing technology. That was The Battery Company's claim to fame.

The laptop computer business was one that I was very familiar with. I hoped that this would be a stepping stone to electric car batteries. Extra manufacturing capacity appeared available in China. That led to partnering with a company in China to manufacture The Battery Company batteries. I asked, on many occasions, whether the technology to manufacture these batteries was compatible with the existing technology for making the common cylindrical batteries as opposed to the prismatic configuration of The Battery Company's model. The answer was always "yes!"

The good news was that my enthusiasm for the improved battery potential and involvement in The Battery Company kept me very busy and took my mind off my pending separation from Thermagon. I truly needed to be busy when I resigned and left the Thermagon premises. Traveling back and forth to Boston was a good thing for me. I had my apartment to furnish and a new city to explore. Also, as chairman of the board, I maintained some level of credibility. I had much to learn about batteries and the world of venture capitalists.

When I started Thermagon, I had only a passing peek at the world of venture capitalists. Suddenly I was learning that the venture capital industry is one big fraternity. The money in the funds they raise comes primarily from men, and the companies that they invest in are run primarily by men. It is hard enough to get venture backing, but as a woman, it was bordering on impossible.

So now you can see why it was such a coup for Christina to receive such backing. However, once they had invested, they commanded a seat on the board and were reluctant to heed any wisdom or advice that came from a woman. A very difficult environment indeed!

I proceeded with the attitude that most anything worth exploring comes with its challenges. It wasn't too long until I began to realize that the pretty pictures and Christina's carefully worded PowerPoint presentations were lacking in substance and verification. Partnering with a company in China to manufacture the batteries was fraught with problems. She very often claimed to be mass producing batteries when, in reality, we were barely limping through a prototype run with the manufacturing parameters in limbo. I made several trips to China on behalf of The Battery Company and saw firsthand the difficulties evolving.

Christina hired a sales manager and then fired him for not making sales. Seems reasonable enough, except she had no batteries to sell. To Christina, a couple of meetings with a company constituted a partnership, so her claims of partnership with prestigious companies were often not so. Company meetings were more like staged screenplays than an open forum for problem-solving.

As the months and years went by, Christina continued to raise money to support her grand research project. I learned that once the original venture money was secured, particularly from a company like Venrock, future investors were less conscientious in their due diligence. Christina was extremely gifted in convincing potential investors to supply money. Even many of the investors I assembled from Cleveland continued to invest money over the next several years.

I began to struggle with backing someone who embellished the truth so much so that it became unclear what was truth and what was fiction. The issue for me was this: When does an exaggeration become an outright untruth? The line was too fine for me, and after two years, I resigned from the board, broke down my apartment in Boston, and had little further contact with The Battery Company. Of course, I hoped for their success and the chance to cash out one day. That has never happened.

When a major Chinese investor came in 2011, Christina cashed out and left the company. Ethical and respectable company founders would have provided their seed investors a path to at least recoup their investment. Not Christina. She moved on without looking back, took her money, and started another company one year later. The new company, as described by Christina, straight from her website states as follows: "The company is poised to become a world leader in battery architecture, performance, safety, with a mission to solve problems through innovation in technology." I certainly recognize the broad, general, flowery language that tells the reader nothing specific about the company. Christina is now known as the "Queen of Batteries." To me, she is the "master of deception." She managed to raise more than $370 million before her exit from The Battery Company.

Christina's exit did not end the endeavors of The Battery Company. The new investors were Chinese and took all but a small office and laboratory in Boston, Massachusetts, to China. One could speculate that all was not lost. However, the new management has refused to recognize the Cleveland contingent of investors as relevant. The company has plodded on with little commercial success. Specific data is not available, and communication with the Cleveland investor group has been denied. The Cleveland contingency is left in limbo, not able to cash out and not able to declare a loss.

If misery loves company, it was not until I became aware of the Theranos story that I realized that the likes of Christina had duped many others more astute than myself. A young woman named Elizabeth Holmes, like Christina, had blond hair and blue eyes and a very engaging personality, started a business in Silicon Valley. Theranos was a company promising to revolutionize blood testing. I became aware of the story of Theranos several years ago, as I was reading the *Wall Street Journal* (*WSJ*). The word Theranos popped off the page, as I had just used their blood testing service out of a Walgreens Drug store in Fountain Hills, Arizona, where I spend my winters. The *WSJ* article was questioning the validity of the Theranos technology. Thank goodness, I had not made any medical decisions based on these results. The *WSJ* article piqued my interest, and I checked out the stories surrounding Holmes and Theranos. Holmes claimed she had come up with a blood test that could be taken with a teeny-weeny drop or two of blood from the finger. This meant that there would be no more searching for a vein and drawing multiple vials of blood with a needle. Her technology was seen as a device to save lives.

The investors she attracted to her company were quite famous in their own right, men such as George Schultz and Henry Kissinger, former Secretary of States, Jim Mattis, current Secretary of Defense, Betsey Devos, current secretary of education, members of the Walton family, and Rupert Murdoch. Overall, Holmes raised in the neighborhood of $900 million and became the darling of Silicon Valley. It was a matter of time before people began to realize that her testing method did not work. She continued to analyze blood by whatever method she could manage while clients were beginning to question her results. In this case, the Theranos laboratory, ultimately, was closed, and the business collapsed.

I tell this story to demonstrate how easy it is to be drawn into a start-up company with a compelling story led by a master salesperson and promoter. I felt very inadequate and gullible to have fallen for The Battery Company story. I brought many of my colleagues along with me. There is some comfort in knowing that others more experienced and knowledgeable than myself have also fallen prey to a fast-talking founder and a convincing story. Unfortunately, there are more stories out there that mimic those of The Battery Company and Theranos. The lesson learned is to beware of company founders whose message is embellished, vague, and sounds too good to be true.

CHAPTER TWENTY-NINE

KEYS TO ENTREPRENEURIAL SUCCESS

You need to spend all of your time and energy on creating something that actually brings value to the people you're asking money for.

—Gary Vaynerchuk

Many books and many experts have expounded on the reasons why start-up businesses succeed or fail. According to Shikhar Gosh of Harvard Business School, 75 percent of venture-backed start-up companies fail, meaning, they never return cash to their investors. Thirty to 40 percent liquidate and go away, and 95 percent never reach their projected return on investment. Venture capital firms rarely own up to these statistics, burying their dead very quietly. Seldom do you see any publicity on failed companies. They just quietly are removed from the venture firm's website. My experiences since Thermagon in engaging with start-up businesses exemplify (follow closely) the Harvard data.

The success or failure of a start-up business can be caused by a myriad of factors acting alone or in tandem. When characterizing entrepreneurs, words like *focus, motivation, commitment, persistence, passion, expertise, listening skills, leadership, financial stewardship, an appetite for risk, market knowledge, customer understanding, team and mentor selection*, etc. come to mind instantly. Most of the entrepreneurs that I have connected with have many of these attributes but still managed to fail. Through the past ten years of engaging with entrepreneurs in the start-up phase, I have concluded that there is one essential attribute that a company must possess to have a chance of being successful. The simplest way to describe this essential ingredient is to say you absolutely must have a competitive advantage.

Let me explain what I mean.

To have a competitive advantage, your company must have at least one of the following three ingredients: a product or service with significantly better performance, lower price, or better customer service. If your company is differentiating itself with a product that fills a market need with significantly improved performance, the improvement probably needs to be greater than 20 percent over the existing competition.

If the differentiation is based on a comparable performance but a lower priced product, the manufacturing process, labor or raw material cost must be significantly lower than the competition. Otherwise, one would never try to compete on price. If the company's business is based on providing a service, differentiation is based on a unique technique for better serving your customers over the competition. Often, success is based on a combination of the above. This implies that you know your market, your customers, you understand how to execute on your operational plan, and you understand your cost and price points relative to the competition. Once you have determined that you have this value proposition, the probability of success increases tremendously. You must ask yourself every day, "Why would a customer select my product or service over the competition?"

What I have found over the past ten-plus years of engaging with founding entrepreneurs is that often the founder is not honest with himself, the investors, and the potential customers about the following: true performance of the product relative to the competition, the actual costs or feasibility to manufacture or any enhanced service value that may exist. In other words, the company CEO kids himself into believing he has a competitive advantage when he does not. Often the founding entrepreneur only reports what he wants to believe or underestimates the competitor's strength. This is not necessarily intentional but is detrimental to the success of the business. You must have tested your products, simultaneously, with the competition's product or have a third party confirm your claims. Performance advantage needs to be greater than 20 percent as a rule of thumb.

For example, the Thermagon products were nearly ten times better in thermal conductivity than any other products out on the market. If you determine that lower cost is your competitive advantage, one might need to engage a cost analyst to determine if the product can be manufactured at a low-enough price to attract customers to your product. This means not only knowing accurately your cost of goods sold but also the price point at which the customers will accept your product. Basing a company's competitive advantage on better service can be harder to quantify and compare to the competition.

For example, at Thermagon, we provided our potential customers with free overnight samples, a service that none of our competitors could duplicate. This function certainly was a factor in our success but was unlikely to provide a differentiating competitive advantage. Service advantage must be compelling enough to drive customers to you and away from your competitors to claim a competitive advantage. This requires an in-depth knowledge of your potential customers' needs and wants. Companies whose product is a service must likewise differentiate themselves from their existing competitors. The founders must find a way to quantify the advantage of their services and clearly communicate them to their potential customers. In all cases, the founder must be able to claim a clear competitive advantage and communicate their value proposition to all constituents. Without this one ingredient, no matter how passionate, hardworking, and intelligent the founder claims to be, he or she will not succeed without a clear and honest competitive advantage.

In Thermagon's case, I had data to demonstrate that the products performed significantly better than the competition, and additionally, I asked each potential customer to please test our products for themselves and determine the performance in their specific application. Also, the products could be manufactured for a price that the market could bear. This required an understanding of the applications into which the products would be placed and how badly they needed the performance advantage that Thermagon could provide. This knowledge governed the product selection and the relative price points. Thermagon service and delivery times were at least equal or better than the competition. In my mind, I told myself that I was not building this company to "turn money," meaning, that I did not want to just breakeven but must make a profit or, in other words, create value. My investors cashed out at forty times their investment. An unbelievable accomplishment!

Every product has a life. It is important to be aware that your competitive advantage will not exist indefinitely. The world is in constant change, and your products and services must adjust to the changes. For example, Thermagon's challenge was to create new products yearly to stay abreast of these changes and maintain their competitive advantage.

As I reflect on the past ten years and all the entrepreneurs with whom I have engaged either through advice or investing, all initially appeared to have the needed ingredients to succeed in their endeavor. Remember that success is based on creating value and returning cash to your investors. In many cases, somewhere in the first couple of years, their claimed competitive advantage could not be sustained. Entrepreneurs reached out to me from a myriad of industries that I have listed below. Of those that still exist, some have succeeded, and others are still developing. Helping entrepreneurs is a labor of love. Taking a technology or idea successfully to market is truly a difficult task. In addition to The Battery Company, I was involved in the following technologies:

- Kinetic energy for charging mobile devices
- Solar arrays
- Process for effectively removing oil from tar sands
- Film technology for improving the display screens in electronics
- Identity-based security architecture for the military

➤ Enhanced software systems for background checks
➤ Battery cooling
➤ Goat cheese
➤ Frozen natural fruit pops
➤ Science projects for preschool children to encourage interest in STEM
➤ Inflatable horse jumps

CHAPTER THIRTY

WHERE'S THE ENGINE?

Enjoy the fruits of your labor.

Despite my experience with The Battery Company, my fascination for electric cars continued. Elon Musk, probably one of the most intelligent and passionate entrepreneurs ever, used mostly his own money to jump start Tesla and develop the completely electric Roadster. I read any and every piece of news about Tesla that I could get my hands on. Few people thought they could succeed, so publicity about their progress was very sparse. In 2008, word came out that Tesla had built a few (probably two) Tesla Roadsters ready to be test driven. The price was claimed to be about $100,000, and they were taking orders so that they could build the first one hundred cars. This meant that you would pay up front and hope that one day you would receive an all-electric Tesla Roadster. Not only did the Roadster look amazing, but it also had specifications claiming to accelerate zero to 60 miles per hour in less than four seconds, have a maximum speed of 125 miles per hour and run 245 miles on one charge. The car was powered by lithium-ion batteries. In the worst way, I wanted to order one of those first one hundred cars. I tried in every way I could imagine to rationalize such a purchase. These cars were being made and sold in California and possibly Arizona into climates quite different from Cleveland, Ohio, where I resided. I knew enough about lithium-ion batteries to realize that climate plays a significant role on their life cycle.

How would I take delivery of the car?

How would I keep it charged?

What if something broke, how would I get it fixed?

The practical side of me began to take over, and then I would tell myself that the car was sure to be a collector's item one day. It was probably not a bad investment. Needless to say, my practical side won out and I refrained from ordering my Tesla Roadster.

By 2010, I had purchased a second home in Fountain Hills, Arizona. All my acquaintances knew that I really liked Tesla. As I was busy renovating my new condo, Doreen, one of my contractors, arrived, claiming she saw a Tesla Roadster parked in the driveway of one of my neighbors. I ran from the condo and down the street in hopes that I would see it before it moved on. Sure enough, there it sat parked in a driveway. That was the first time I had ever seen a real one. Only slightly reluctantly, I stepped up to the door and rang the bell. I had no idea who lived there. An elderly lady answered, and I immediately exclaimed, "It's a Tesla! It's a Tesla!"

She looked at me startled and probably thought I was a lunatic. She then said the car belonged to her son. I stared blankly. I think she began to realize that I was not going to leave until her son showed me the car. He finally came out, showing very little enthusiasm and emotion. He spoke with me for a few minutes about the car, and that was my first real-life encounter with a Tesla. Tesla had already begun the development of a four-door sedan. It was called the Model S. By 2011, the beta Model S was introduced. Sometime in the next couple of years, a Tesla showroom appeared in the Fashion Square mall in Scottsdale, Arizona. By 2012, Tesla had stopped making the Roadster. So one day, when I wandered into the Fashion Square Mall, it was the Model S that was on display. It was absolutely beautiful! I knew more than most (women) about the specifications of the car and the battery pack. The young salesmen touting the attributes of the car were quite taken back with my knowledge and enthusiasm.

That day, I settled on the purchase of a Tesla hat. It wasn't until fall of 2015 that I ordered my actual Tesla, the only car that ever intrigued me. It was the technology in the car, the freedom from the dependence on oil, and the pleasurable buying experience that made the difference. I had waited just long enough to allow Tesla to work out the start-up bugs with the car and to receive the software for autonomous driving. The driving experience is amazing! So amazing that my neighbor who oversees my car while I am in Ohio, fell in love with it, and has now acquired his own Tesla.

CHAPTER THIRTY-ONE

MOMENTS OF PRIDE

To be honored is to exceed one's expectations.

Margaret Heffernan, author of the book *How She Does It* once again used my entrepreneurial experience in her article in *More!* magazine titled "In Good Company." In the article, she explains why midlife women make superior entrepreneurs. She used my story to disprove the myth that entrepreneurs have to be young and that you must have heaps of cash to succeed.

Margaret asked me to speak to one of her classes at Simmons College, a small liberal arts college for women in the center of Boston. The astonished look on the students' faces as I was introduced was worth noting. How could I be an entrepreneur at my ripe old age of sixty-seven? I told my story, and the students were convinced that "being young was not a prerequisite for being a successful entrepreneur."

The greater Cleveland community became aware of Thermagon's involvement in the inner city with the creation of the beautiful space on West Forty-Fifth Street and our many employees who reside in the inner city. When Bill Strickland came to Cleveland promoting his brilliant model for an internationally recognized arts and education center for disadvantaged students and adults, I was asked to be one of his interviewees. You can learn more about Bill Strickland through his book *Make the Impossible Possible: One Man's Crusade to Inspire Others to Dream Bigger and Achieve the Extraordinary*. Strickland spent the last thirty years transforming the lives of thousands of people through his company Manchester Bidwell, a jobs and training center and community arts program in Pittsburgh. Strickland had come to Cleveland to help create a similar program for Cleveland.

On meeting Bill Strickland, I sensed that he had serious doubts about my ability to understand his work and message. In the course of the interview, I was able to convince him that through my work at Thermagon, I had firsthand knowledge of the inner city and was keenly interested in his mission. I became part of the founding board of the Cleveland Center for Arts and Technology, now called New Bridge, a nonprofit start-up. The transition from for-profit start-ups to nonprofit start-ups was educational and rewarding for me. We started by finding a building to renovate and proceeded from there to create a fantastic center with the help of Cleveland Foundation, Cleveland Clinic, and many others. New Bridge provides innovative arts programs for at-risk students after school and during the day provides workforce training for at-risk adults at no cost to the students. As with all start-ups, it was not without its challenges. I have since turned my board seat over to others in the community, but I am proud today of their many successes. For more information, see www.newbridgecleveland.org. Much of the art you will see in the beautiful space created in the center is the work of my daughter, Diane, and is on loan from the Latham family.

The YWCA Greater Cleveland believes that women leaders shape our communities. As part of their mission dedicated to eliminating racism; empowering women; and promoting peace, justice, freedom and dignity for all, the YWCA has established the Women of Achievement Award. The award is one of the most prestigious honors for women in Northeast Ohio, honoring women who embody outstanding leadership qualities, are exceptionally committed to their careers and communities and live the YWCA mission. I believe that it was not only my success with Thermagon but also the community work with New Bridge that drew the attention of the YWCA. In 2011, I was honored by being one of the five Women of Achievement for that year!

A most humbling experience!

It was not until these post-Thermagon years that I rediscovered my alma mater, Ohio Wesleyan University (OWU). OWU, founded in 1842, is committed to liberal arts education, diversity, and service. My belief that a college education should teach students how to think and solve problems rather than being simply vocational training has attracted me back to OWU to support their excellent program for preparing students to be leaders in a global society. Their emphasis on providing theory to practice experiences for the students anywhere in the world piqued my interest.

My initial reconnection was through the economics department and the Woltemade Center (the Center) for economics, business, and entrepreneurship. I joined the Alumni Advisory Board and shared the Thermagon story with economics classes and served as a mentor to students.

In partnership with the economics department, the Center, among other tasks and responsibilities, provides generous scholarships, meaningful internships throughout the world, an outstanding lecture series, a living/learning environment for upper-class students, and the Economics Management Fellows (EMF) Program for especially able incoming first-year students with an interest in economics and business. The success of this EMF Program enhanced the stature of the Center and energized the alumni board. The EMF program is highlighted by a five-day study tour of New York City, where the students are hosted by OWU alumni. While visiting their businesses, the students learn much about the financial and business aspects of each company. As a result of this program, interest grew to create other programs that would enhance the students' experience, particularly for upperclassmen. Statistics showed that students who participate in this program have a higher retention rate and greater overall success. As interest grew to create other programs, an administrative director was added to the team to help make this happen.

Meanwhile, I was invited to be a trustee of OWU and sit on its board, an honor indeed. With this honor comes significant responsibility. The role of the board in implementing the OWU mission include responsibilities such as managing and overseeing the president, ensuring financial integrity, overseeing and participating in fund-raising, defining and differentiating OWU's program, and providing necessary fiscal, physical, and human resources to meet present and future need. In today's world, the value of a college education is being challenged as never before. Trustees are faced with the role of helping the university maintain its enrollment and contain its costs.

Applying my entrepreneurial experiences to the success of a university has been very challenging. Small liberal arts colleges like Ohio Wesleyan University are faced with a declining market, increased expenses, and a decrease in government grants. Maintaining and growing enrollment is a constant challenge. Creating and maintaining a competitive advantage has become exceedingly difficult. As a trustee and board member, it becomes more and more imperative that one understands the programs and student experience of the competition to differentiate themselves from the pack.

As I reflected on the issues for attaining a competitive advantage for OWU, on the impact that I could make through my financial commitment to them, and on my personal goals, I came up with an idea on how to build synergy. My idea was to create an entrepreneurship program that would have the potential to differentiate the university, as well as provide me with the means to fulfill my lifetime goal of promoting and supporting entrepreneurship through a philanthropic gift to OWU. From this idea, we created the Latham Entrepreneurial Scholars Program (ESP). Through the leadership of the Center, the university is launching the interdisciplinary ESP for students seeking to become the next generation of trailblazers. The program, a two-year commitment for sophomores and juniors, is interdisciplinary by my design and engages students from all majors, disciplines, and backgrounds across campus. I believe that through unexpected combinations and crossing boundaries one achieves surprising results. Where but at a small liberal arts college could this goal be so effectively met? The course curriculum will be taught using professors across all the disciplines of the university.

Additionally, all ESP students will complete an internship with an entrepreneurial focus and receive a stipend to help support their experience. OWU has just dedicated a building to house the Entrepreneurial Center, a collaboration between Delaware County, city of Delaware, and OWU. This collaboration is a prime example of crossing boundaries to create something extraordinary. Entrepreneurial interest is surging, and I could not be more excited. I hope that students for many years hence, will be able to take advantage of this creative program and, in so doing, will create a competitive advantage for the whole university. I plan to share the proceeds from the publishing of this book with the Latham Entrepreneurial Scholars Program at Ohio Wesleyan University.

Over the years, I maintained a blind eye toward the prospects of receiving honors or awards. Each time I was contacted with news of being selected for recognition, I had a complete reaction of surprise and disbelief. Each time I was recognized, I felt certain that this would be the last. When I received the phone call last year from Rock Jones, President of OWU, informing me that I had been selected by the Ohio Foundation of Independent Colleges to be inducted into their Hall of Excellence, I was completely speechless and totally surprised.

I was one of two to be selected for 2018, joining a prestigious group of Ohio Independent College alumni honored since 1987. This Hall of Excellence honors individuals who have attained positions of leadership in their professional careers, demonstrated exemplary civic engagement, and, in the spirit of the liberal arts tradition, taken paths of lifelong learning and supported independent higher education in Ohio. As I glanced over this list of individuals in the Hall of Excellence, names like Hugh Downs, ABC News Anchorman; Bobby Rahal of car racing fame; Ralph Regula, member of the US House of Representatives; as well as a multitude of chairman and CEOs of major US corporations came to my attention.

How could this be? I pondered. Rock assured me this was real. As I hung up the phone, I was stunned. As I prepared my remarks and assembled family members and close friends, this Evening of Excellence was a most memorable occasion. I was certain that this is the last time.

CHAPTER THIRTY-TWO

LAIRD TODAY

If the result is that someone, somewhere winds up believing they can do something out of the ordinary, well, then you've really made it.

Knowing that Thermagon, the company that I founded, nurtured, grew, and ultimately sold, continues to thrive within the Laird Technologies umbrella gives me a strong sense of pride. All too often acquired companies are misunderstood, mismanaged, and left to dissolve within the parent company's regime. I feel very fortunate that Laird did not follow this pattern. Laird, on the other hand, was determined to be in the thermal materials business. After acquiring Thermagon, Laird proceeded to purchase other thermal materials businesses that complimented the Thermagon technology. Needless to say, Laird dramatically changed Thermagon, creating many challenges and opportunities for those involved.

Over the nearly fifteen years under Laird supervision, sales of thermal materials grew more than fourfold. This is a far cry from extinction. They manage employees across the globe. The resources generated provided career opportunities for many employees. Today the Cleveland-based part of the performance material business employees about sixty-five people. That compares to about eighty employees at Thermagon at the time of the sale. About one quarter of the current employees remain from the Thermagon days. I have had informal discussions with most all of them over the past month, and I commend them for overcoming the challenges and becoming a major force in the Laird success. I believe that today they remain the brains behind the accomplishments of the Laird thermal business. I am proud of each and every one of them.

Those employees who were leaders in operations or technology found channels for advancement as part of a larger company. Some became vice presidents, some became directors, and some became managers or group leaders, enhancing their wages, their stature, their knowledge, and their experiences. Many have had travel experiences that may never have occurred as part of Thermagon. They talked with enthusiasm about their travels to Asia, Europe, Mexico, and far parts of the United States. Some employees declined offers to travel to China. Understanding that all people are not comfortable with such extensive international travel, Laird was understanding and did not penalize those who declined their offers. Some said when they attended thermal meetings and met with contemporaries or customers, if they identified themselves as from Thermagon rather than Laird, they received immediate respect and recognition. This is confirmation that Thermagon was truly a technical leader in thermal materials.

Even though there was a dramatic culture change for the employees working under Laird management, Laird continued the Thermagon commitment to provide educational university programs to employees at their expense. Many employees have taken advantage of these opportunities. Employees participated in everything from two-year educational certificates of accomplishment to master's degrees in science.

Understandably, a few found little comfort or reward under the new regime. They all seem proud that they have endured the many changes and challenges over the past fifteen years. However, they yearn for the Thermagon days when the culture was quite different. In my discussions, I heard many times that Thermagon was like a family who cared about their well-being. The existing environment was more typical large corporation where the average employee is a means to an end rather than a real person. Many expressed a concern about the future of their jobs. I tried to encourage them and assure them that their loyalty and seniority would help them in future decisions. Jobs and employment do not come with guarantees. Some talked about the frequent changes in management and the stress caused. Some acknowledged that communication was sketchy and felt very detached from the big picture or strategy. Despite their frustration, they treasured their knowledge and skills in the thermal business, and down deep they knew they made a positive difference in the day-to-day operations of Laird. A change in technology leadership and the recent return of Jim, my oldest son, promises to provide an organization that will maintain Laird as the technology leader in thermal materials.

The most significant change that came to Thermagon after the acquisition resulted from Laird's commitment to globalization, which refers to the process by which technological, economic, political, and cultural exchanges made the world a more interconnected and interdependent place. In the business world, this includes increased trade and investment flows, currency exchange, and the rise of multinational corporations. Communication and transportation technologies are capable of linking people who are physically distant from one another, thereby facilitating the exchange of culture, knowledge, and ideas. Technological advances, including mobile phones and particularly the internet, have contributed to globalization by connecting people all over the globe. The World Wide Web links billions of people and devices, providing innumerable opportunities for the exchange of goods, services, cultural products, knowledge, and ideas.

By 2004, the year of the Thermagon acquisition, massive globalization was already in progress. Laird had already moved much of its manufacturing to China, securing engineering expertise and factory space. Additionally, the computer and telecommunication equipment manufacturers representing a large portion of the Thermagon customers were already manufacturing their equipment in China. This provided the added advantage of producing the thermal materials closer to the customers. As you have guessed, Laird purchased Thermagon with the intent to move much of the manufacturing to China. The inevitable happened. Piece by piece and product by product, the manufacturing of the thermal materials moved to China.

This globalization movement created many positive and negative outcomes. To create the potential to produce materials at lower costs is a very large and positive reason to manufacture in China. Labor was plentiful and definitely cheaper in China. Lower manufacturing costs could not only make the products more competitive but could also enhance corporate profit. The short-term gains were nearly impossible to pass up.

On the other hand, this movement caused millions of Americans to lose manufacturing jobs from 2001 to 2010. Job loss was estimated to be six million or one-third of all United States manufacturing employment. For Thermagon/Laird, the percentage was even greater, estimated to be around 70 percent. Currently, about eighteen people have manufacturing jobs at Laird in Cleveland.

As if the loss of American manufacturing jobs would not be reason enough to be concerned about transferring manufacturing to China, the transfer of intellectual property and trade secrets has become increasingly apparent and worrisome in recent years. That a small company like Thermagon could become a prime example of the effects of American job loss, and the loss of intellectual property seems incredible to me. One can only imagine the effects on many multibillion-dollar companies who have lost American manufacturing jobs, compromised much of their technology, and yet improved profitability, at least in the short term. In my informal interviews with current Thermagon/Laird employees, I heard several times that while at electronics conferences, employees would be thanked by small Chinese thermal material companies for having taught them the art of making good performing materials. This is how that works.

Cleveland employees would go to China and teach the Laird Chinese operators how to make the once Thermagon materials, as well as the new Laird materials. Once they became proficient in their skills, these Chinese operators would quit their jobs and start their own business.

Waa la!

Laird now had a new competitor. It is true that usually these Chinese companies did not have the brand recognition, the quality systems, or the development skills to create new materials. Competing for them could be difficult. That is assuming that they don't just make "knockoffs" and pass them off as Laird products.

Now fifteen years since the sale of Thermagon, news on the national front is peppered with reports of technology loss, computer hacking and military collaboration involving China. Micron Technology Inc., the United States's largest memory chipmaker, has sued Fujian Jinhua Integrated Circuit Company for stealing their intellectual property and trade secrets. Jinhua is a semiconductor start-up into which the Chinese government has been pouring money, as part of an effort to build its own chip industry. The United States Commerce Department has restricted American firms from doing business with them. Such retaliation was rare several years ago.

In another instance, scientists from the Chinese military are collaborating with scholars from United States universities. In some cases, the Chinese scientists masked their ties with the Chinese military, enabling them to work with professors of leading universities like Carnegie Mellon. In other news, United States federal prosecutors have charged Chinese intelligence officers of hacking information-technology service providers for espionage and intellectual property theft.

The Chinese technology giant, Huawei, is the world's largest maker of telecommunications equipment, the number two maker of smartphones worldwide and a major customer of Laird for thermal materials. Huawei is currently facing a United States criminal probe for allegedly stealing trade secrets from US business partners, including technology used by T-Mobile. This is in addition to other United States scrutiny, which has led to the effective blocking of the company from installing its telecommunications equipment in major US networks for fear its gear could be used to spy on Americans. Other American pressure on Huawei has led to the arrest in Canada of Huawei chief financial officer Meng Wanzhou, daughter of the company founder, Ren Zhengfei. She is accused of misleading banks about the nature of Huawei's business in Iran, leading to violations of United States sanctions on the country. Fears of such activities have led to Chinese divestments of large US corporations, including

McDonald's Corporation, Hewlett-Packard Co., Cardinal Health, and Visteon. The list goes on and on.

My personal interaction with China and the Chinese people was nothing but positive. Henry Paulson, with both Goldman Sachs and then as Treasury Secretary for George W. Bush, was an enthusiastic champion of the United States's engagement with China. Nonetheless, Mr. Paulson became critical of China's direction. According to a November 2018 article in the *Wall Street Journal*, he claimed that now, seventeen years after China joined the World Trade Organization, it still "has not opened its economy to foreign competition in so many areas," using joint venture requirements, ownership limits, technical standards, subsidies, licensing procedures, and regulation to block foreign competition.

"This is simply unacceptable."

Who is to say where the future will take us? Globalism is an ideology that is struggling with the current move toward patriotism/nationalism. Will the collateral damage that breakneck globalization has inflicted on our ordinary workers and on our intellectual property loss be reconciled in the years to come?

You decide!

ABOUT THE AUTHOR

Taking discoveries from the idea phase to a successful product in the marketplace became Carol Latham's passion. She developed her own unique technology for producing high thermal conductivity materials used to cool the chips in computers and other electronic systems. Her company, Thermagon Inc., became an international success in the nineties and was sold to Laird Technologies in 2004. Laird continues to be successful in manufacturing and marketing the thermally conductive materials that Carol created.

Carol, as a graduate of Ohio Wesleyan University (OWU) and a strong proponent of a liberal arts education, currently serves on the OWU Alumnae Board of the Woltemade Center for economics, business, and entrepreneurship and as a trustee of the university.

Carol recently created an entrepreneurial scholar's program, a multidisciplinary two-year commitment for students selected from all departments of the university with the intent of advancing their ability to become successful entrepreneurs.

Carol strove to boost the quality of life, not only for her employees but also for residents in the intercity. At Thermagon, located in the near west side of Cleveland, she hired unskilled people, mostly women, from the surrounding neighborhood. While at Thermagon, these women received skill-enhancing training that served to further their careers. Additionally, she served as a founding board member for the creation of the Cleveland Center for Arts and Technology, New Bridge, an organization charged with the task of changing the lives of at-risk students and economically disadvantaged adults in the Cleveland area.

Carol has three adult children and five grandchildren. She is an avid sports fan, loves to play tennis, enjoys classical and jazz music, and collects contemporary art.

CPSIA information can be obtained
at www.ICGtesting.com
Printed in the USA
BVHW062051240120
570268BV00006B/59